The Common Core Grammar Toolkit

Using Mentor Texts to Teach the Language Standards in Grades 3–5

Sean Ruday

Eye On Education
6 Depot Way West, Suite 106
Larchmont, NY 10538
(914) 833–0551
(914) 833–0761 fax
www.eyeoneducation.com

For information about permission to reproduce selections from this book, write:
Eye On Education, Permissions Dept., Suite 106, 6 Depot Way West, Larchmont, NY 10538.

Library of Congress Cataloging-in-Publication Data

Ruday, Sean.
The common core the grammar toolkit : using mentor texts to teach the language
standards in grades 3–5 / by Sean Ruday.
    pages   cm
Includes bibliographical references.
ISBN 978-1-59667-247-5
1. English language—Grammar—Study and teaching (Elementary)
I. Title.
LB1576.R776 2013
372.61—dc23   2013004301

10 9 8 7 6 5 4 3 2 1

Sponsoring Editor: Robert Sickles
Production Editor: Lauren Davis
Copyeditor: Kathleen White
Designer and Compositor: Matthew Williams, click! Publishing Services
Cover Designer: Dave Strauss/3FoldDesign

Also Available from EYE ON EDUCATION

Vocabulary Strategies That Work:
Do This—Not That!
Lori G. Wilfong

Common Core Literacy Lesson Plans:
Ready-to-Use Resources, K–5
Edited by Lauren Davis

Assessing Critical Thinking in Elementary Schools:
Meeting the Common Core
Rebecca Stobaugh

Helping English Language Learners Meet the Common Core:
Assessment and Instructional Strategies, K–12
Paul Boyd-Batstone

Vocabulary at the Core:
Teaching the Common Core Standards
Amy Benjamin and John T. Crow

Rigor Is Not a Four-Letter Word, Second Edition
Barbara R. Blackburn

Awakening Brilliance in the Writer's Workshop:
Using Notebooks, Mentor Texts, and the Writing Process
Lisa Morris

Teaching Grammar:
What Really Works
Amy Benjamin and Joan Berger

Guided Math in Action: Building Each Student's
Mathematical Proficiency with Small-Group Instruction
Dr. Nicki Newton

Strategies for Common Core Mathematics:
Implementing the Standards for Mathematical Practice K–5
Leslie A. Texas and Tammy L. Jones

Using Formative Assessment to Drive
Mathematics Instruction in Grades 3–5
Christine Oberdorf and Jennifer Taylor-Cox

Supplemental Downloads

An annotated bibliography, containing examples from literature used in this book, is available on Eye On Education's website as an Adobe Acrobat file. In addition, blank versions of the charts and templates in this book are available on Eye On Education's website as Adobe Acrobat files. Permission has been granted to purchasers of this book to download these resources and print them.

You can access these downloads by visiting Eye On Education's website: www.eyeoneducation.com. From the home page, click on "Free," then click on "Supplemental Downloads." Alternatively, you can search or browse our website to find this book, then click on "Log in to Access Supplemental Downloads."

Your book-buyer access code is CCG-7247-5.

Bonus Download
Annotated Bibliography With Literary Examples

Table of Contents

Meet the Author

Sean Ruday is Assistant Professor of English Education at Longwood University. He began his teaching career at a public school in Brooklyn, New York and has taught English and language arts at public and private schools in New York, Massachusetts, and Virginia. He holds a BA from Boston College, an MA from New York University, and a Ph.D. from the University of Virginia. His articles have appeared in *Journal of Language and Literacy Education*, *Contemporary Issues in Technology and Teacher Education*, *American School Board Journal*, and *Virginia English Bulletin*. Sean is a frequent presenter at regional and national conferences. He enjoys talking with teachers about innovative ways to improve students' literacy learning. You can follow him on Twitter @SeanRuday. His website is seanruday .weebly.com. This is his first book with Eye On Education.

Acknowledgments

I would like to thank the teachers who contributed to this book by allowing me to include their ideas, insights, and classroom practices. I learned a great deal from each one of those wonderful educators.

I would also like to thank the students whose works are included in this book. I loved seeing how those students improved their writing by mastering and incorporating key grammatical concepts.

In addition, I want to thank the staff of Eye On Education, especially Senior Editor Lauren Davis. I am extremely appreciative of Lauren's continued support of this project, from its beginning stages to its final form.

I also want to thank my parents, Bob and Joyce Ruday, for the countless ways they've supported this book and all of my other endeavors.

Finally, I want to express an incredible amount of gratitude to my wife, Clare Ruday, for the happiness and encouragement she provides me on a daily basis.

What's in Your Toolkit?
Connecting Literature and Grammar Instruction

The momentum was about to shift, and Rachel[1] knew it. Her fourth-grade students were engaged in a writing lesson, working intently on memoirs of meaningful events in their lives. However, she knew she needed to instruct them on some grammatical concepts with which they had been struggling. "I knew I was going to lose them," explained Rachel. "They were writing about their lives and were totally engaged, but the minute I said *pronoun* or *preposition*, they were going to zone out." Rachel, a recent student in a college-level course I teach about grammar instruction in the K–12 classroom, is not alone in her observation that grammar instruction has the potential to disengage even motivated students. Traditional grammar exercises, taught out of context or not included in writing instruction, frequently reduce student interest levels (Woltjer, 1998) and have very little impact on student writing (Weaver, 1998).

These research findings ran through my head during my conversation with Rachel. The Common Core State Standards emphasize grammar and language study, but how can teachers devise grammar instruction that keeps students engaged *and* makes them better writers? This important question does not affect just Rachel and other isolated teachers but also represents a key concern relevant to the instructional practices of literacy teachers around the country. Given the challenges of grammar instruction and the degree that the Common Core Language Standards value proficiency in specific grammatical concepts, I believed it was important to write this book. It is intended to be a resource for teachers seeking ways to address the challenges Rachel and countless others face: teaching grammar in ways that engage students, ensure their understandings of key concepts, and help them become better writers.

This book focuses on grammar instruction that promotes metacognition of grammatical concepts. It provides teachers of third, fourth, and fifth graders with recommendations for grammar instruction that help students develop an understanding of how and why authors use certain grammatical concepts. The grammatical concepts discussed come from the Common Core Language Standards that relate to grammar instruction in the third, fourth, and fifth grades. This book seeks to help teachers use literature in their classes to illustrate the importance of these grammatical concepts, with the ultimate goal of engaging students in critical analysis of how grammar is used in young adult and children's literature. In this approach,

All names used in this book were changed.

students read a work of age-appropriate literature and analyze how and why the author made the grammatical choices that he or she did. Doing so enhances students' metacognition of grammatical concepts by discussing how they can improve writing and how a piece of writing might be different if other grammatical concepts were used.

This introductory chapter consists of the following components:

- A discussion of why literature is a useful tool for studying grammar
- An explanation of the importance of metacognition to students' awareness of grammatical concepts
- A discussion of the gradual release model and why it's important to grammar instruction
- An overview of what to expect in the rest of the book, including the grammatical concepts addressed in the upcoming chapters

Literature: The Entryway to Innovative Grammar Instruction

The National Council of Teachers of English explains the importance of viewing reading and writing as related entities:

> Writing and reading are related. People who read a lot have a much easier time getting better at writing. In order to write a particular kind of text, it helps if the writer has read that kind of text. In order to take on a particular style of language, the writer needs to have read that language, to have heard it in her mind, so that she can hear it again in order to compose it. (NCTE Beliefs about the Teaching of Writing, 2004)

This relationship between reading and writing is at the heart of this book's approach to grammar instruction. To teach students specific grammatical concepts, teachers must show them how to look at that concept from a writer's perspective. The NCTE recommends that teachers understand "how writers read in a special way, with an eye toward not just what the text says but how it is put together" (NCTE, 2004) and then give their students the skills to do this as well. Such instruction can limit the disconnect between grammar instruction and writing that Weaver (1998) describes; if students see how authors use these tools in their writing, students can begin to think about how they can do the same in their own work.

For example, in a discussion about prepositional phrases, I would show elementary school students an example of literature in which an author used prepositional phrases to enhance a piece of writing. We would talk about what effect the prepositional phrases had on the piece, how those phrases enhanced the writing, and what the piece would be like with the prepositional phrases removed. A possible example is the excerpt that follows:

> On a silver dish in front of Billy lay an ice-cream cake bathed in fruit syrups—peach, cherry, tutti-frutti, candied orange—topped with whipped cream sprinkled with jelly beans and almond slivers.
>   "It's called a Whizbang Worm Delight," said Billy's mother proudly. "I made it up."
>   "Is the worm really in there?" said Billy, poking about with his spoon. And then, scraping away a bit of whipped cream at one end, he glimpsed the worm's snout protruding from the center of the cake" (Thomas Rockwell, *How to Eat Fried Worms*, 1973, p.77.)

By identifying the prepositional phrases in the text and considering what they add to the piece, students can begin thinking about the writer's "toolbox": specific strategies or tools that writers use to achieve certain objectives. Just as a writer might use an engaging lead that begins in the middle of the action or a sensory image for a specific purpose, she or he might also use a grammatical concept such as a prepositional phrase to achieve a particular goal. As students begin to consider the reasons writers use certain grammatical concepts, they move toward thinking metacognitively about grammar.

Metacognition: What's in Your Toolkit?

Metacognition has a bit of an intimidating sound. As one of the elementary school teachers with whom I have worked put it, "Metacognition sounds way too scientific. Is this really something I should talk about with my students?" In a word: absolutely! Metacognition, knowledge of cognitive phenomena (Flavell, 1979), is often thought of as thinking about thinking (Garner, 1987). In the context of grammar instruction, metacognition can mean understanding why a writer might use a certain grammatical concept and what effect the use of that concept might have on a piece of writing (such as in the example with prepositional phrases). Helping students achieve this understanding can allow them to see aspects of grammar as tools instead of simply as terms that need to be memorized and then forgotten.

To introduce the idea of metacognition to young writers, I begin by asking students to think of some specific examples of tools. As they call out such tools as hammer, screwdriver, and chainsaw (a favorite of upper-elementary and middle-school boys), I write the tool names on a piece of chart paper. We discuss what the different tools do and why someone might use them. I then state that writers use tools as well and explain that we will explore a variety of strategies that writers use to achieve certain goals. I write on the board, "What do a chainsaw and an adverb have in common?" Some students laugh; others raise their hands. Sometimes it takes a bit of scaffolding, but we discuss the ideas in the question until we arrive at the point where the class understands that grammatical concepts are tools that writers use for specific purposes, just as craftspeople use tools to achieve particular objectives. A mechanic wouldn't use a hammer when a screwdriver is needed (at least I hope not!), and a writer wouldn't use an adverb in place of an adjective. Each is a tool with a purposeful use.

I tell young writers that they will read pieces of literature but will do so in different ways than they have previously done. Instead of reading solely for ideas such as plot and character, they will be reading for tools by looking at the ways authors use aspects of grammar to enhance their works. I explain that they will learn grammar but that we will discuss it in ways that are probably different than the ways they've previously done so: analyses of literature and discussions of why authors do what they do will replace work sheets. After we look at how published authors use these concepts, I tell the students that we will talk about ways they can use these aspects of grammar to improve their writing. Throughout this process, students think about their thinking: they reflect on their analyses of literature as well as on how they use key grammatical concepts in their own writing. As students analyze the grammatical tools published writers use and apply those concepts to their own works, they become increasingly metacognitive thinkers who can confidently state what chainsaws and adverbs have in common.

Comments from a fifth-grade boy named John provide insight into what thinking metacognitively about grammar can mean to student writing:

> I had never heard of relative clauses before, but now I know how writers use them and that they add important information. In my story, I said, "Boris, who was the scariest man I ever met, came to my door." The relative clause, "who was the scariest man I ever met," shows a lot about Boris and adds important details. I liked reading books with relative clauses because that showed me how to use them.

John's explanation of relative clauses reveals his understanding of relative clauses as a tool that writers use to add details to their work. He shows that he understands the concept as both a writer and a reader, reflecting on his experience reading books that contain relative clauses and analyzing a specific relative clause used in a piece of his writing. John's analysis reveals that this concept is now part of his writer's toolbox from which he can draw in his future work.

The Gradual Release Model of Instruction

Grammar instruction can be especially effective when teachers gradually release the amount of responsibility students take for the concepts being taught. In this instructional model, called the gradual release of responsibility (Pearson and Gallagher, 1983), teachers initially model the use of a grammatical concept, work on examples with the students, and then ask the students to work independently when they are ready to do so. For example, in a lesson on pronoun reference, a teacher could begin by delivering direct instruction on what pronoun reference is, using examples to illustrate the main points. After this, the teacher could provide students with more responsibility by working on some examples with them. For instance, the teacher could show students some example sentences and discuss with them whether the sentences contain clear pronoun references. Once the teacher is comfortable with the students' understandings of the topic, she or he could "turn them loose" to work independently or in small groups. In this instance, the teacher might ask the students to examine their own pieces of writing, looking for clear pronoun references. Finally, the teacher might conclude the lesson by asking students to reflect on why pronoun reference is important to good writing.

Note that, in this lesson example, responsibility for the learning activities moved from being solely on the teacher to being primarily on the students. In this book, you'll find many examples of grammar lessons that incorporate this model, which has been shown to improve students' reading comprehension (Lloyd, 2004) and writing achievement levels (Fisher & Frey, 2003). When utilizing the gradual release model with your students, be aware that not all the steps have to take place in one day or class period. You might use one language arts period to model and explain a concept to your students, another to work on examples with them, and then a third to give students opportunities for independent practice. The amount of time you and your students take should depend on their needs and your assessment of their understandings.

What to Expect in This Book

This book was designed to be a guide for grammar and writing teachers in the new era of Common Core Standards. It focuses on metacognition of grammatical concepts that helps students grow as both readers and writers and takes its focal concepts from the Common Core Language Standards for grades three, four, and five. The remainder of the book is organized into four sections, each containing multiple chapters that address topics important to that section:

- ◆ Grammatical concepts aligned with Grade Three Common Core Language Standards
- ◆ Grammatical concepts aligned with Grade Four Common Core Language Standards
- ◆ Grammatical concepts aligned with Grade Five Common Core Language Standards
- ◆ A final section called "Putting It Together." It describes methods of formative and summative assessment that can be used to gauge students' understandings of these concepts as well as a

conclusion, which contains some final thoughts and tips for class-room practice.

Available for free download is an annotated bibliography, which lists the works of children's and young adult literature featured in the book, a key grammatical concept found in each work, and the Common Core Language Standard associated with that concept.

The following table lists the grammatical concepts in the book, the chapters in which they are discussed, and the Common Core Language Standards with which they align.

Grammatical Concept	Chapter	Common Core State Standard
Pronoun Reference	Chapter 1	L3.1
Subject-Verb Agreement	Chapter 2	L3.1
Using Commas and Quotation Marks in Dialogue	Chapter 3	L3.2
Simple, Compound, and Complex Sentences	Chapter 4	L3.1
Differences Between Spoken and Written English	Chapter 5	L3.3
Relative Pronouns and Relative Adverbs	Chapter 6	L4.1
Progressive Verb Tenses	Chapter 7	L4.1
Modal Auxiliaries	Chapter 8	L4.1
Prepositional Phrases	Chapter 9	L4.1
Capitalization Use	Chapter 10	L4.2
Choosing Words and Phrases to Convey Ideas Precisely	Chapter 11	L4.3
The Perfect Verb Tenses	Chapter 12	L5.1
Conjunctions and Interjections	Chapter 13	L5.1
Using Punctuation for Clarity and Effect	Chapter 14	L5.2
Dialects and Language Variations	Chapter 15	L5.3
Figurative Language	Chapter 16	L5.5

In each chapter, we'll take a "boots on the ground" approach by exploring specific strategies and activities teachers can use to introduce students to these grammatical concepts, improve metacognition of them, and enable students to apply the concepts to their own writing. We'll read about the practices of classroom teachers who have used these activities and learn from their experiences teaching grammar in these ways. Each chapter is organized into the following sections for consistency and ease of use:

- ♦ An overview of the nuts and bolts of the chapter's focal concept
- ♦ A discussion of why the concept is important to good writing, including examples of how published authors use the concept in their own works
- ♦ A classroom "snapshot" that describes an exemplary instance of a particular teacher working with students on the chapter's focal concept
- ♦ Some specific instructional recommendations for teachers to use when teaching the concept to their own students

The Classroom Snapshot

A few words about the classroom snapshot sections: each describes one of three teachers. The snapshots in chapters 1 through 5 describe Ms. Jay's experiences teaching her third-grade class, those in chapters 6 through 11 focus on Ms. Walker's work with her fourth graders, and those in chapters 12 through 16 chronicle Ms. Fernandez' instruction of her fifth graders. The teachers possess certain similarities and differences. All of them teach at the same school and worked with me as I consulted with the school's faculty and administration on grammar instruction. I talked with these teachers about the instructional methods described in this book and supported them as they implemented and mastered these methods.

Ms. Jay was in her fifth year of teaching when I worked with her; she had previously read, when studying for her master's degree, information about teaching grammar in the context of writing instruction, which gave her some background on the instructional practices described here. Ms. Jay is a very lively, spirited teacher; you'll notice her frequent use of the phrase "Rock on!" to praise student work.

Ms. Walker was in her tenth year of teaching when she taught the lessons described in this book; although she was not very familiar with the instructional practices when we first started talking about them, she grasped the ideas quickly and naturally. She knew she wanted her students to understand grammar in ways that went beyond memorization, and these practices certainly served that purpose.

Ms. Fernandez was in her third year of teaching when she taught the lessons described here. When we started working together, she explained that she understood grammar well but had learned it in more traditional ways, such as through using textbooks, completing work sheets, and diagramming sentences. Although she was initially more comfortable teaching as she had been taught, she wanted to give her students the kind of instruction that would maximize their successes and therefore tried out the methods described in this book. She did an excellent job incorporating this instructional approach and saw great improvements in her students' work.

I describe the range in these teachers' backgrounds and styles to show that all teachers, regardless of their previous experiences and levels of familiarity with connecting grammar, literature, and writing instruction can implement the practices described in this book and use them to facilitate their students' successes.

If you're ready to learn more about innovative ways to connect grammar instruction and the Common Core Language Standards with metacognition and literature, keep reading!

Section 1

Grammatical Concepts Aligned With Grade Three
Common Core Language Standards

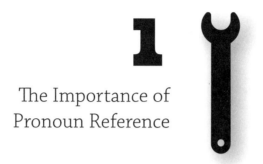

1

The Importance of Pronoun Reference

What Is Pronoun Reference?

Common Core Language Standard 3.1 addresses the importance of pronoun reference, emphasizing "pronoun-antecedent agreement" as part of a more general standard that states students should "demonstrate command of the conventions of standard English grammar and usage when writing or speaking" (Common Core Standards, 2010). When talking with students about pronoun-antecedent agreement, I like to use the term "pronoun reference," as it highlights the most important aspect of this concept: pronouns must clearly refer to particular antecedents. If a piece of writing does not have clear pronoun reference, readers will get so bogged down in trying to make sense of what a particular pronoun refers to that they can lose all sense of the narrative.

Pronoun reference problems appear in all kinds of situations; when talking with a group of third graders about their Halloween adventures, I heard this example: "Josh went as Darth Vader for Halloween, and Dan dressed up like Yoda. His costume was awesome." In this situation, the pronoun *his* was problematic; I didn't know if it referred to Josh's costume or Dan's. Because the pronoun did not clearly refer to a particular antecedent, the audience was bound to be confused. I wanted to fully listen to more about the Halloween adventures of Josh and Dan, but the unclear pronoun reference distracted me.

Figure 1.1 (page 4) summarizes some key points regarding pronoun reference.

Figure 1.1 Information About Pronoun Reference

Grammatical Concept	Pronoun Reference
What is pronoun reference?	Pronoun reference refers to clear agreement between pronouns and antecedents. Writers need to make sure that pronouns clearly refer to particular antecedents.
What are some examples of clear pronoun reference?	1. Brody and Sawyer are going to the baseball game. **They** are wearing **their** new hats. 2. Julie is at soccer practice. **She** is wearing new shoes.
Why are these examples correct?	• In the first example, *they* and *their* are plural pronouns that correctly refer to the plural subject *Brody and Sawyer*. If the writer had used a singular pronoun, there would be a problem because the reader wouldn't know which antecedent the pronoun referred to. • In the second example, the singular pronoun *she* is a correct example of pronoun reference because that pronoun agrees with the singular subject *Julie*. As is the case in this example, writers may need to check for gender and number when ensuring proper pronoun reference.

Why Pronoun Reference Is Important to Good Writing

When discussing pronoun reference with students, I emphasize the importance of this concept to good writing. Writing without clear pronoun use can confuse readers and make it impossible for readers and the writer to share a common understanding of what's taking place. It's best if students can think of this concept as a tool of effective writing that helps readers fully engage in a piece of writing instead of being confused by its pronouns. I like to illustrate the importance of clear pronoun reference by using the works of published authors. By calling attention to the ways those authors use pronouns and why clear pronoun use helps those pieces make sense, students can understand why this concept is important to good writing.

The following example, from Mary Pope Osborne's novel *Sunset of the Sabertooth*, contains clear pronoun reference: "Annie held the rope with both hands. She pushed her feet against the side of the pit. She rose into the air with the rope" (Osborne, 1996, p. 45). The pronoun reference in this passage is clear because it's obvious to readers that *she* refers to Annie each time it is used. Although this may seem obvious, that's because Osborne used pronoun reference correctly; when the pronoun reference in a passage is unclear, it's extremely hard to decipher what's happening in a sentence.

If Osborne's piece read, "Annie held the rope with both hands. She pushed her feet against the side of the pit. **They** rose into the air with the rope," the piece would be quite different. Instead of focusing on the action in the piece, readers would find themselves asking questions such as "Whom does *they* refer to? Isn't this just about Annie? Are there other characters involved that I've missed?"

Another example from *Sunset of the Sabertooth* further illustrates the importance of clear pronoun reference to effectively communicate meaning. Early in the novel, readers learn that "Eight-year-old Jack and his seven-year-old sister, Annie, climbed into the tree house. They found it was filled with books" (p.1). This passage tells us that Jack and Annie did these things together; they both climbed into the tree house and discovered the books. This information is important to the novel, as the book goes on to describe the many adventures Jack and Annie had together. If the passage about the siblings climbing into the tree house instead read, "**She** found it was filled with books," the passage would take on a very different meaning. Instead of showing Jack and Annie finding the books together, the text would indicate that only Annie did so, leaving readers to ask what Jack was doing and why only Annie found the books.

As these examples from Osborne's novel illustrate, clear pronoun reference is important because it allows readers to understand what's taking place in the text. In the next section, we'll look at how Ms. Jay helps her third graders understand how pronoun reference can play a major role in good writing.

A Classroom Snapshot

It's early in the school year in Ms. Jay's class; it's still hot outside, and students have just returned from recess. As the excited third graders find their spots on the carpet that serves as the class's meeting place, they see Ms. Jay standing next to an easel pad. The phrase "Pronoun Reference: A Tool for Clear Writing" is written across the top. Ms. Jay has contemplated this lesson for a while. Her students are working on memoirs, in which they focus on particular events from their lives that strike them as especially meaningful.

When I met with Ms. Jay before class, she showed me the students' drafts: One student is writing about playing basketball with his older brothers, another's piece describes her most recent family reunion, and another is writing about her experience riding a roller coaster for the first time. Ms. Jay thought this would be an effective way to open the school year because the students could share meaningful experiences. "It's going well," she shared with me, "but I'm not sure what do about pronouns. I know they've learned about pronouns, and they can definitely pick them out from grammar workbooks and things like that, but they confuse them a lot in their writing."

Ms. Jay explained what she was seeing: "One girl was writing about playing volleyball with her friends. She used the pronoun *she*, but there was no way to tell which friend *she* was referring to. I know [this student] understands what pronouns are and can do lots of grammar book exercises with them, but she isn't able to clearly use them in her writing." I nodded; pronoun reference errors such as these are common in student writing. In fact, errors in pronoun reference have been identified as the second most common grammar mistake in college writing (Connors & Lunsford, 1988). Because clear pronoun-antecedent agreement is part of the grade-3 Common Core Language Standards, teachers need to ensure that students master it at a young age so they don't continue to struggle with it.

Ms. Jay's observation that her students can demonstrate mastery of pronoun reference in grammar book activities but not necessarily in their writing aligns with research that indicates that out-of-context textbook work does not improve students' abilities to apply grammatical concepts in their own writing (Weaver, 1998). She and I brainstormed ways to help her students apply the concept of pronoun reference to their writing. We needed to come up with ways to help develop the students' metacognition of the concept; in other words, we wanted them to be aware of what clear pronoun reference is, why it's important to effective writing, and how they can ensure it is present in their work, both now and in the future.

Let's return to Ms. Jay's work with her class and see how she makes her students aware of the importance of pronoun reference. Now that her students have settled into their assigned squares on the class carpet, they listen as she introduces the topic: "OK, y'all. Let's get going! Take a look at what I've written here: Pronoun Reference: A Tool for Clear Writing. Can someone tell us what a pronoun is?"

Student hands shoot up and Ms. Jay calls on one student to provide an explanation: "Words you say when you don't say someone's real name—*he* or *she*."

"Rock on!" replies Ms. Jay. "Pronouns are tools that writers use when they don't want to say nouns' actual names. Pronouns take the place of nouns." Ms. Jay goes on to explain that pronouns are important because they can help writers avoid being repetitive. "If you were writing about me, you wouldn't want to say 'Ms. Jay, Ms. Jay, Ms. Jay' over and over again. That would be soooo boring!" The students laugh. "You could say *she* to make it less repetitive," Ms. Jay continues. "Even though pronouns are really good for this reason, they can also be tricky. Writers who use pronouns need to make sure readers can tell whom pronouns are talking about. That's pronoun reference. Let me show y'all what I mean."

Ms. Jay turns the large pad of paper on the easel pad to reveal the following text, which she has transcribed from Louis Sachar's novel *Sideways Stories from Wayside School*: "Joe had curly hair. But he didn't know how much hair he had. He couldn't count that high" (Sachar, 1985, p. 19). She reads the text aloud to the class and asks, "What are the pronouns?" Students raise their hands, identifying the different examples of the pronoun *he* in the text, all of which refer to the antecedent *Joe*. Ms. Jay commends their efforts and then asks, "What if we changed one of these pronouns? Would the passage make sense?" The students look around, presumably wondering how the passage would read with different pronouns. Ms. Jay then provides her next instructions: "Y'all get together with your partners (the students in this class have assigned partners for pair assignments such as this one) and make a change to this passage: rewrite it, but change at least one of these *he* pronouns we've picked out to a different pronoun."

The students move to the tables in the classroom, working with their assigned partners to rewrite the passage with a changed pronoun. Ms. Jay checks in with various pairs, nodding thoughtfully as they show her their work. Once she is satisfied, Ms. Jay returns to her place on the carpet and asks the students to come together and share their work. Students volunteer to share their sentences and point out which pronouns they replaced; as they do this, Ms. Jay writes the sentences on the easel pad and discusses with the class how the sentences' meanings have changed. One volunteer shares: "Joe had curly hair. But he didn't know how much hair he had. **She** couldn't count that high." Ms. Jay asks the student how this passage differs from the original text, to which the student responds: "Well, we changed the last *he* to *she*, so now it's saying that a girl couldn't count that high."

Ms. Jay smiles, pleased with this response, and comments further: "The meaning's very different now, isn't it?" Students nod as she continues: "When the pronoun was *he*, we could assume that *he* referred to *Joe*. Now that the last pronoun is *she*, we know there's a girl or a woman who couldn't count that high but we don't know who that is, whom the pronoun refers to or is talking about. This is why pronoun reference is so important. If pronoun reference isn't clear, readers can get really confused."

Another student volunteers a different revision: "Joe had curly hair. But **it** didn't know how much hair he had. **It** couldn't count that high." Again, Ms. Jay follows up by asking the student how this new example varies from the original text. The student replies, "We changed two of the *he*s to *it*s. It's not the same anymore, because the sentence is talking about an *it*."

"The pronoun *it* sure does make the sentence different!" responds Ms. Jay. "I know it makes me wonder what *it* is referring to."

"Maybe a monster!" shouts one student, as others laugh

"Yes, maybe a monster," smiles Ms. Jay. "One thing we definitely know is changing that pronoun really makes a difference in the meaning of this piece of writing. When you write, make sure that the pronouns you use clearly match up with what they're replacing." She turns back to the piece of chart paper headed Pronoun Reference: A Tool for Clear Writing and asks a student volunteer to explain why pronoun reference is a tool for good writing. A number of students' hands go up. The first one whom Ms. Jay calls on offers her thoughts: "If the pronouns are confusing, you might not really know what's going on."

Ms. Jay is pleased with the response: "Rock on! This is an important tool for making sure your writing makes sense." She tells the students that she'll be conferencing with them about their memoirs and discuss pronoun reference in their work.

As the students begin the writing workshop portion of their day, Ms. Jay sits down with individual students for writing conferences. She focuses on pronoun reference and asks the students to explain which nouns specific pronouns refer to. Later that week, Ms. Jay follows up to let me know how her students are doing with pronoun reference. "Their writing is so much better," she explains. "Their pronouns are clear, and they understand why certain mistakes are wrong. They finally understand how to do this in their writing." Ms. Jay's response suggests that her students have increased their metacognition of this concept; their understanding of what pronoun reference is and why it's important has allowed them to finally translate this concept to their written work.

Recommendations for Teaching Pronoun Reference

In this section, I described a step-by-step instructional process I recommend teachers use when teaching about pronoun reference. This process was designed to help students understand the importance of pronoun reference and apply that understanding to their writing. I organized it into the following parts:

1. Present the use of pronouns as a tool for clear writing.
2. Provide models of clear pronoun reference.
3. Ask students to change some of the pronouns.
4. Help students analyze the changes.
5. Ask students to apply this concept to their own writing.

This process was designed to help students take an active role in understanding pronoun reference; instead of simply being told of the importance of this concept, they can change pronouns in existing models, examine differences in the sentences, and apply the concept to their own work. Depending on the time you have available and your students' needs and characteristics, you can spread the lesson's components over multiple days or conduct the whole lesson at one time.

1. Present the use of pronouns as a tool for clear writing.
I recommend beginning by describing why using pronouns is an important tool for clear writing. In my experience, third-grade students frequently understand what pronouns are but often have little to say when discussing why they are important to effective writing. To help students understand why good writers use pronouns, I recommend focusing on two key components: (1) Pronouns eliminate repetition, and (2) pronouns are effective

only if a piece of writing has clear pronoun reference. I suggest starting a mini-lesson on reviewing basic information about pronouns; this is the starting point for the more advanced discussions of pronoun reference that will follow.

As Ms. Jay did in her lesson, opening the conversation by talking with students about what pronouns are and why writers use them as a way of avoiding repetition is a good idea. This allows the students to think about the pronouns they use and see in everyday life. After establishing this background on pronouns, the next step is to make the connection to pronoun reference by talking about what a piece of writing would be like if its pronoun reference was unclear. Because pronoun reference can sound like an abstract concept to third graders, the best way to help students understand it is to show them concrete examples, such as those described in the next section.

2. Provide models of clear pronoun reference.
Providing models of clear pronoun reference makes this grammatical concept more concrete to students and helps them fully grasp its importance. I recommend showing students examples from literature so that they can see how published authors use pronouns in their works. Asking students to talk about how published authors use grammatical concepts such as pronoun reference helps students understand why these concepts are important to good writing; instead of seeing pronoun reference as a mistake to fix, students can learn to view this concept as an important part of good writing. The sentence that Ms. Jay used from Sachar's book *Sideways Stories from Wayside School* is an excellent example of this. Because this passage contains so many examples of the pronoun *he*, it is well-suited for a class discussion of pronoun reference. Teachers and students can discuss how each *he* clearly refers to *Joe*; if other pronouns were used or if the passage referred to more than one person, it would be unclear whom *he* was referring to.

3. Ask students to change some of the pronouns.
I recommend asking students to intentionally make a piece of writing unclear by changing some of its pronouns. Asking students to work with an excerpt from a published text can help them understand that pronoun reference is a tool implemented by professional writers to ensure their work is clear and logical. Without it, readers would be confused and pay more attention to this confusion than to the information in the piece.

4. Help students analyze the changes.
The passages students generate in these activities purposely do not contain clear pronoun reference. What the passages do provide, however, is an excellent opportunity for analysis; I recommend asking students to think about the differences in the passages and ways those distinctions

illustrate the importance of clear pronoun reference. This final reflection helps teachers make sure students have grasped the focus of the lesson and lets teachers emphasize the importance of clear pronoun reference to effective writing.

To engage the students in this kind of analysis, I like to present them with the following reflection questions:

- Which pronouns did you replace? What did you replace them with?
- How do the new pronouns change meaning?
- What questions might readers ask when reading the new piece you created?

To give my students support and clear expectations, I model this activity with another passage before asking them to discuss theirs. I've found that modeling my own analysis first gives students an understanding of what I expect and guards against confusion and anxiousness. Because many students haven't had experience analyzing how and why authors use grammatical concepts, it's a good idea to provide a clear framework before beginning the activity. For example, I've modeled this kind of analysis with the following passage from Bruce Hale's detective novel *The Big Nap*: "The next day we'd have to start beating the bushes for another case. But first we'd savor the end of this one" (Hale, 2001, p. 109). When conducting this activity, I alter this passage to read "The next day we'd have to start beating the bushes for another case. But first **she'd** savor the end of this one," intentionally confusing the pronoun reference.

Following are the responses to the analysis questions I share with my students while I model this activity:

- Which pronouns did you replace? What did you replace them with?
  "I replaced the second *we* in this passage with *she*."
- How do the new pronouns change the meaning?
  "The pronoun *she* changes the meaning because it makes the passage say something completely different. Instead of saying that **we** would savor the end of the case, it refers to a **she** and says that **she** will savor the end of it. This creates a whole new situation."
- What questions might readers ask when reading the new piece you created?
  "Readers would definitely ask who **she** is and why **she** is the only one savoring the end of the case. Readers might want to know if something happened to make it so that **she** is the only one savoring it."

After I finish modeling my analysis, my students have a clear understanding of what kind of analysis I'm looking for. Armed with these clear expectations, students can apply their analytical skills to the counter examples they created. By analyzing the changes they made to the original text, students can enhance their understanding of why pronoun reference is an important tool for clear and effective writing.

5. Ask students to apply this concept to their own writing.
Once this analysis is complete, students can return to their own work and confidently edit for clear pronoun reference. Their enhanced understanding of this concept allows them to use this tool in their own work. We saw this idea in practice in Ms. Jay's class; after she talked with the students about how their changed sentences differed from the original passages, she conferenced with individual students about pronoun reference issues. Students who have thought critically about the importance of clear pronoun reference know that checking for pronoun-antecedent agreement is a tool that writers use to ensure they're clearly communicating with their readers. After you discuss this topic with your students, they'll be well-positioned to do the same.

Final Thoughts on Pronoun Reference

The information below summarizes major points from this chapter, including what this grammatical concept is, why it's important for good writing, and how one might teach it for maximum effectiveness.

- ◆ Clear pronoun reference is included in Common Core Language Standard 3.1.
- ◆ Pronoun reference refers to clear agreement between pronouns and antecedents.
- ◆ A piece of writing with confusing pronoun reference can distract readers and result in confusion regarding who is performing the action in the piece.
- ◆ When teaching pronoun reference, ask students to do these four things:
  - Examine models of clear pronoun reference.
  - Replace the pronouns in those examples and intentionally create pronoun reference errors.
  - Analyze the differences.
  - Apply the concept of clear pronoun reference in their own writing.

Subject-Verb Agreement

What Is Subject-Verb Agreement?

Common Core Language Standard 3.1 calls for students to "ensure subject-verb . . . agreement" when writing and speaking (Common Core Standards, 2010). The essence of subject-verb agreement is that singular subjects have singular verbs, and plural subjects need plural verbs. This concept, although logical, has the potential to be problematic for students. To apply the rule to their own work, students need to understand the ways verbs can change when nouns and pronouns change from first- or second- to third-person point of view and from singular to plural.

The tense of a sentence makes a difference as well; a sentence written in the past tense uses a different form of a verb than one written in the present. For example, the sentence "She runs on the track" is written in the present tense, while "She ran on the track" is written in the past tense. Each one of these sentences contains subject-verb agreement, but the specific verb form used varies based on whether the sentence is written in the past or present tense.

In addition, students need to understand various irregular verbs that can make mastering subject-verb agreement especially challenging. Killgallon and Killgallon (2010) refer to verbs as the tools of narration; to be clear and effective narrators, students need the skills to make sure that subjects and verbs agree. The major topics to address when discussing subject verb agreement are first-person narration, second person narration, third-person narration, and irregular verbs. Each concept is crucial to students' abilities to clearly depict the events taking place in their works.

First-Person Narration

In first-person narration, the narrator performs the action. This narrative style produces easy subject-verb agreement: the verb stays the same whether the subject is singular or plural. However, the actual verb used varies based on whether the sentence is in the present tense or past tense. Here are two sentences written in the present tense that use first-person narration, one with a singular subject and one with a plural one:

> **Singular:** At school, I *learn* about pirates.
> **Plural:** At school, we *learn* about pirates.

Even when the subject changed from singular to plural, the verb *learn* remained the same. The next sentences also use first-person narration and are in the past tense. As you can see, the verbs in these sentences remain the same when the subject changes from singular to plural:

> **Singular:** I *learned* that pirates enjoy dancing.
> **Plural:** We *learned* that pirates enjoy dancing.

Second-Person Narration

In second-person narration, the narrator is speaking directly to the reader, often using the pronoun "you." While this style of narration is not as common as first- and third-person narration, it is still an important concept for students to grasp as they make sense of subject-verb agreement. Since "you" is both a singular and plural pronoun, sentences in second-person narration typically contain the same verb form whether they refer to individuals or groups. Below are two of the sentences from the previous section, revised to include second-person narration. You'll notice that they are identical. The only reason one would be singular and the other plural would come from the context in which the sentences are used; the "singular" sentence would refer to one student, while the "plural" sentence would refer to a group of students.

> **Singular:** At school, you *learn* about pirates.
> **Plural:** At school, you *learn* about pirates.

Similarly, sentences that use second-person narration and are in the past tense do not change verb forms whether they're referring to one person or more than one. In the sentences below, the first would refer to a singular person and the second to multiple people, but the sentences themselves are written identically:

> **Singular:** You *learned* that pirates enjoy dancing.
> **Plural:** You *learned* that pirates enjoy dancing.

Third-Person Narration

In third-person narration, someone other than the narrator performs the action. This narrative style contains a bit more variation than first- and second-person narration: verbs in the present tense change their forms based on whether the subject is singular or plural, but verbs in the past tense do not. Because of this variation, we'll look at third-person narration in the present tense and then examine it in the past tense.

Third-Person Narration in Present Tense

In the third-person, present tense, verbs change forms when they change from singular to plural by dropping the *s* at the end, as in the two sentences below:

> **Singular:** The pirate *dances* to hip-hop music.
> **Plural:** The pirates *dance* to hip-hop music.

Note that the first sentence has a singular subject (pirate) and a verb with an *s* at the end (dances). This verb form is called the third-person singular and is typically formed by adding an *s* to the end of the word. In the second sentence, the subject is plural (pirates) and the verb does not include the final *s* (dance). This verb form is called the third-person plural and uses the verb's base form—in other words, the verb without anything added to the end.

Third-Person Narration in Past Tense

When a piece is narrated in the third-person past tense, verbs don't make the same transformation based on whether the subject is singular or plural. Let's put the dancing pirate sentences in the past tense:

> **Singular:** The pirate *danced* to hip-hop music.
> **Plural:** The pirates *danced* to hip-hop music.

Notice the difference? In each sentence, the verb remains *danced*, whether the subject is singular or plural. Each verb takes on the past tense (typically formed by adding *ed* to the end of the verb) regardless of the number (singular, plural) of the subject.

Irregular Verbs

As if the variation between past and present tenses isn't enough, the issue of subject-verb agreement is further complicated by irregular verbs. Unlike the forms of the verb *dance* in the previous examples, irregular verbs deviate from standard verb patterns. Irregular verbs are important to master, as they are frequently used in daily communication; in fact, the ten most frequently used English verbs are irregular (Kolln & Funk, 2009). However, irregular verbs don't need to stand in the way of students' mastering

Figure 2.1 Examples of *Be*

Forms of the Verb *Be*			
Point of View	**Tense**	**Number**	**Example**
First person	Present	Singular	I *am* dancing.
First person	Present	Plural	We *are* dancing.
First person	Past	Singular	I *was* dancing.
First person	Past	Plural	We *were* dancing.
Second person	Present	Singular	You *are* dancing.
Second person	Present	Plural	You *are* dancing.
Second person	Past	Singular	You *were* dancing.
Second person	Past	Plural	You *were* dancing.
Third person	Present	Singular	She *is* dancing.
Third person	Present	Plural	They *are* dancing.
Third person	Past	Singular	She *was* dancing.
Third person	Past	Plural	They *were* dancing.

subject-verb agreement. Because so many of the most common English verbs are irregular, students already have a great deal of familiarity with these verbs, even if they aren't yet aware of it. According to Kolln and Funk, the verb *be* is the most frequently used English verb as well as the most irregular—it has the most variations on its basic form. The table in Figure 2.1 (above) illustrates various forms of the verb *be* based on the point of view of the narration, the tense of the sentence, and the number of subjects.

Why Is Subject-Verb Agreement Important to Good Writing?

Subject-verb agreement is an important tool for creating clear and effective writing. If students use plural subjects with singular verbs, or singular subjects with plural verbs, their writing will be hard to decipher. In such situations, readers are likely to be confused about what action is taking place and the number of people who are performing it. On the other hand, a piece with strong subject-verb agreement allows readers to easily envision what the author intended. Subject-verb agreement is similar to the issue of pronoun reference described in the previous chapter; if these tools are used effectively, readers can fully engage in a particular piece of writing and understand the situation taking place in the work. If pronoun reference is unclear or subjects and verbs don't agree, readers will spend more time figuring out what the author meant to say than enjoying the piece.

To illustrate the importance of subject-verb agreement, it's helpful to look at the impact it has on published writing, such as this example from Susan Sharpe's novel *Trouble at Marsh Harbor*: "By ten in the morning, **Matt** and **Ben** *were* at the fairgrounds" (Sharpe, 1990, p. 46). Note that the sentence's subjects, **Matt** and **Ben**, are in bold, and the verb, *were*, is in italics. The agreement between the sentence's subjects and its verb allows readers to clearly understand what's taking place: there are two subjects in the sentence, and both of them were at the fairgrounds. If the sentence changed to "By ten in the morning, **Matt** and **Ben** *was* at the fairgrounds," the meaning would be unclear. If I came across that sentence in a piece of writing, I would be confused and hesitant. I would ask myself if Ben was the only one at the fairgrounds and, if so, what Matt was doing. I would wonder if I had missed something earlier in the story that clarified this situation or if it was just a case of subjects and verbs not agreeing.

Without clear subject-verb agreement, readers may ask themselves anxious questions such as the ones I posed above. I like to tell my students that readers expect a lot from authors: readers want to be entertained, but they also want a clearly told story that eliminates unnecessary confusion. After all, a lack of clarity can ultimately result in a lack of enjoyment; confused readers won't marvel at a writer's skillful description, engaging plot, or well-developed characters. Instead, the readers will try to figure out what is actually taking place. During a conversation with a group of third graders about subject verb agreement, I asked the students why they thought subject-verb agreement was important to effective writing and recorded their responses on the piece of chart paper pictured in Figure 2.2 (page 18).

These responses reveal the students' understanding of subject-verb agreement as a useful tool for effective writing. Without clear subject-verb agreement, the positive attributes they describe—clear, enjoyable writing on which readers can easily focus—would be much harder to achieve.

Let's look at Ms. Jay's third-grade classroom and check out the creative instructional methods she uses to help her students understand subject-verb agreement.

A Classroom Snapshot

Ms. Jay's students are understandably surprised. They have just sat down on the carpet that serves as the class's meeting space when she tells the students she's going to show them a picture of Superman. Her third graders look quizzically at her, wondering if this could possibly be related to the language arts instruction they typically have at this time in the school day. Ms. Jay explains that, after she shows the picture of Superman, she's going to talk about what Superman is doing. "I'm going to use

Figure 2.2 Why Is Subject-Verb Agreement Important?

Why is subject—verb agreement important?

- Makes writing clear
- Helps readers enjoy your writing
- Keeps readers from getting distracted

the present tense when I do it," she explains. "When I use the present tense, I say what's happening right now." She shows the students a picture of Superman in the air and thinks aloud about what she sees: "I see Superman in the air, and it looks like he's flying, so I'm going to say, 'Superman flies through the air.' I'm going to write that sentence on our paper here," she explains as she writes "Superman flies through the air" on a large piece of chart paper that rests on an easel pad.

Next, Ms. Jay pulls out another picture. This one depicts both Superman and an airplane in the air. "This one has both Superman *and* an airplane. If I wanted to describe what's happening here, I wouldn't say 'Superman and an airplane flies through the air.' I would say 'Superman and an airplane *fly* through the air.'" She writes "Superman and an airplane fly through the air" underneath the previous sentence so that students can see the differences in them.

"Look at these sentences, y'all," she states. "What's different about them?" Initially, students hesitate to respond, so Ms. Jay directs their attention to the differences in the verbs, explaining that the first sentence contains a singular subject—*Superman*—and the verb in that sentence is flies. The second sentence has a plural subject—*Superman* and *an airplane*—and the verb in that sentence is *fly*. "Notice how the verb changes there?" Ms. Jay asks. "This is called subject-verb agreement, and it's really important for clear writing. The verb in the sentence has to match the number of subjects, or readers can really get confused. If I said, 'Superman and an airplane *flies* through the air' instead of *fly*, it would sound weird and confusing. It might be hard to tell which one was actually flying."

Ms. Jay turns to the next page of chart paper, which reads "Singular subjects need singular verbs. Plural subjects need plural verbs." "This is the main point of subject-verb agreement," she asserts. "Sometimes a verb form is different depending on whether the subject is singular or plural. Writers need to use the correct form so readers don't get confused."

Next, Ms. Jay illustrates the way a sentence's tense can influence its subject-verb agreement. She explains that if the sentences about Superman and the airplane were in the past tense, the verb would not change. "If those sentences were in the past tense, they'd sound like this: The first one would say 'Superman flew through the air.' The second one would be 'Superman and an airplane flew through the air.' That verb didn't change, did it?" Students shake their heads. Ms. Jay continues, "It's *flew* in both sentences. It stays the same. In the past tense, a lot of verbs will be the same whether the subject is singular or plural, as *flew* was here."

Ms. Jay transitions to the next part of the lesson by explaining that a good way to learn about what good writers do is to look at good writing. "I know y'all love the *Diary of a Wimpy Kid* books," she says. "So we're going to look at some sentences in those books and pay attention to the subject-verb agreement." Ms. Jay picks up the book *Diary of a Wimpy Kid*, opens it to a page that she has already marked with a post-it note, and places that page on the document projector so it is displayed in the front of the room for the class to see. She directs the class's attention to the sentence: "Dad walked down to the basement to chew Rodrick out, and I tagged along" (Kinney, 2007, p. 12). Ms. Jay tells the students that the first step to looking at the subject-verb agreement in a sentence is identifying the subjects and verbs. She then asks if any of the students can point out the subjects and verbs in the sentence. Hands sprout up all over the room; Ms. Jay calls on the first student to raise her hand, who correctly identifies *Dad* as the subject of the sentence and *walked* as the verb.

"Rock on!" replies Ms. Jay. "Now, what if the sentence had a plural subject of *Dad and Mom* instead of just *Dad*? What would the verb be then?" The students are initially quiet; some look over at the statement on the chart paper to see if that might give them a clue. Ms. Jay tries to jog their memories: "Remember when we said, 'Superman and an airplane flew through the air?' Did the verb change?" Prompted by this, a student raises her hand and comments, "If the subject was *Dad and Mom*, the verb would still be *walked* because it's in the past tense."

"Rock on!" responds Ms. Jay. "Here is another example from *Diary of a Wimpy Kid*." She turns to another page from the book and displays it on the document projector so that the following text is featured: "Dad really hates heavy metal, and that's the kind of music Rodrick and his band play" (Kinney, 2007, p. 31). She asks the students to identify the subject and verb in the first part of the sentence, and volunteers quickly identify *Dad* as the subject and *hates* as the verb. After Ms. Jay commends their efforts, she again asks students to think about what the verb would be if the subject changed to *Dad* and *Mom* or another plural subject. "Go ahead and rewrite the sentence," she says, "and change the subject to *Dad and Mom*. Think about what the best verb would be." After the students write, Ms. Jay asks a volunteer to share a rewrite. Many hands go up; the student Ms. Jay calls on states, "Dad and Mom really hate heavy metal, and that's the kind of music Rodrick and his band play."

Ms. Jay smiles from ear to ear. "Rock on!" she responds. "Can you tell us why the verb changed?" The student explains that because the subject was plural, the verb had to change, as in the example with Superman and the airplane. Ms. Jay states that this is an excellent start on subject-verb agreement and praises the students: "You already sound like pros at it!"

Recommendations for Teaching Subject-Verb Agreement

In this section, I describe an instructional process for teaching subject-verb agreement, which consists of the following steps:

1. Find examples of subject-verb agreement in literature.
2. Explain why subjects and verbs agree in the examples.
3. Ask students to consider how changes to sentences affect the sentences' subject-verb agreement.
4. Talk with the students about how subject-verb agreement makes writing effective.

These steps were designed to help increase students' understandings of why clear subject-verb agreement is instrumental to good writing and ways writers use this concept in their work.

1. Find examples of subject-verb agreement in literature.
When I spoke with Ms. Jay after her lesson, she told me she felt using examples from *Diary of a Wimpy Kid* made the lesson especially effective. "That showed [the students] that this is something that is used in their favorite books. It helped engage them and helped them learn." As Ms. Jay's response suggests, finding examples in literature makes the material more relevant for students, especially if it's done with age-appropriate texts that the students enjoy. In addition, it helps the students see the concept being studied (in this case, subject-verb agreement) as an important tool for writing, not just something to be memorized and forgotten. Therefore, I strongly recommend teaching subject-verb agreement by finding examples of it in high-interest published works. It's best to find a few different styles of narration with different kinds of subject-verb agreement. For example, Ms. Jay used one sentence in the past tense of the third-person singular and one in the present tense of that same form. This helped the students analyze the text and see what this concept looks like in practice.

Figure 2.3 Subject-Verb Agreement Model Chart

Book	Text Excerpt	Subject	Verb	Explanation of Subject-Verb Agreement
Flat Stanley: Stanley and the Magic Lamp, by Jeff Brown	"Mr. Lambchop served three more balls . . ." (Brown, 1983, p.63).	Mr. Lambchop	served	This sentence has a singular subject. The sentence is in the third person and the past tense, so the verb *served* is the same whether the subject is singular or plural.

2. Explain why subjects and verbs agree in the examples.

Once you've shown students some examples of subject-verb agreement from a published work, I recommend working with them to explain the examples. The amount of scaffolding students will need to successfully complete this activity will vary based on how well students are grasping the concept and how challenging a particular example of subject-verb agreement may be; a sentence with an irregular verb will require more explanation than a more straightforward example, such as a regular verb in the past tense. Think back to the gradual release model discussed in the introduction; as students become more comfortable with subject-verb agreement, you can release more responsibility to them and allow them to complete activities independently.

Figure 2.3 (above) is an example of a chart I use to help my students explain examples of subject-verb agreement.

After I show my students this example and discuss it with them, we work on one together. Finally, I give them a blank example of this chart, which they can fill out with excerpts from novels of their choice. This releases the responsibility to the students and allows them to gradually take more ownership of their learning. A blank example of the chart is available as a supplemental download for your own use (see page iv).

3. Ask students to consider how changes to sentences affect subject-verb agreement.

The next step in this process is to ask students to consider what the subject-verb agreement in particular sentences would be like if something about the sentence was changed. Recall how Ms. Jay asked her students to consider what a sentence from *Diary of a Wimpy Kid* would be like if the subject was *Dad and Mom* instead of only *Dad*. Asking students to think about whether the verb form would change if the sentence had a plural subject requires them to think critically about the sentence's subject-verb agreement. There are a number of ways to engage students in this kind of interpretation; to facilitate this, I ask students to consider topics such as the number of subjects, the tense, and the point of view of the narration.

I recently helped a group of third graders conduct this kind of analysis using the example from *Flat Stanley: Stanley and the Magic Lamp* (Jeff Brown, 1983) discussed in Figure 2.3. Groups of students were instructed to alter the number of subjects, the tense, or the point of view in the original text— "Mr. Lambchop served three more balls . . ."—and explain whether the form of the verb needed to be changed. One group changed the number of subjects in the sentence to create the text "Mr. and Mrs. Lambchop served three more balls," which did not affect the form of the verb. Another group altered the tense of the sentence so that it read "Mr. Lambchop serves three more balls"; this change does require a change in the form of the verb, illustrating that changing the sentence's tense can alter the verb needed in the sentence. This activity is most beneficial when students consider the reasons a verb *does* or *does not* change in an alternative version of a sentence. Doing so can help students further understand the reasons behind certain changes made to verbs and help them apply those principles to their own writing.

4. Talk with students about how subject-verb agreement makes writing effective.

Finally, I recommend having a closing conversation with the students about how subject-verb agreement makes writing effective. To conduct this conversation, look back at the literary examples you've discussed and ask the students to comment on how subject-verb agreement makes the sentences easy to understand. You can also have students look at their own writing, find examples of subject-verb agreement, and comment on why a piece would be confusing if the subjects and verbs did not agree. Conversations such as these can help students understand that subject-verb agreement is an important tool for clear and effective writing.

Final Thoughts on Subject-Verb Agreement

The information below summarizes major points from this chapter, including what the grammatical concept is, why it's important for good writing, and how one might teach it for maximum effectiveness.

   ◆ Subject-verb agreement is included in Common Core Language Standard 3.1.
   ◆ The essence of subject-verb agreement is that singular subjects take singular verbs, and plural subjects need plural verbs.

- ◆ To be clear and effective narrators, students need to make sure the subjects and verbs in their writing agree.
- ◆ Three major topics to address when discussing subject-verb agreement are first-person narration, third-person narration, and irregular verbs.

When teaching about subject-verb agreement, ask students to do these four things:

- ◆ Find examples in literature.
- ◆ Explain how the subjects and verbs in those examples agree.
- ◆ Consider how changes to sentences would affect the sentences' subject-verb agreement.
- ◆ Think about how subject-verb agreement makes writing effective.

Using Commas and Quotation Marks When Writing Dialogue

What Does "Use Commas and Quotation Marks When Writing Dialogue" Mean?

Common Core Language Standard 3.2 addresses the way students punctuate the dialogue in their writing. As part of a more general statement that students should "Demonstrate command of the conventions of standard English capitalization, punctuation, and spelling when writing," this standard calls for students to "Use commas and quotation marks in dialogue" (Common Core, 2010).

This element of Standard 3.2 means that students need to follow certain guidelines regarding comma and quotation use when punctuating the dialogue in their writing. These guidelines are important because they clearly separate a speaker's words from the rest of the piece. To explore these guidelines in detail, let's look at some examples of correctly punctuated dialogue and then examine what makes them correct.

Authors use four typical sentence patterns when writing dialogue. The differences in these patterns have to do with the placement and presence of the "speaker tag," which is the part of the sentence that identifies the speaker—for example, Ben said.

Pattern One: The Sentence Begins With the Speaker Tag

In the first pattern, the sentence begins with the speaker tag: Ben said, "I think we're going to win the game tonight." In this sentence, there is a comma after the speaker tag. The quotation marks show readers exactly what Ben said; therefore, the opening quotation mark is placed before the word *I* and not before the speaker tag. It's important to note that the closing quotation mark at the end of the sentence is placed after the period.

Pattern Two: The Sentence Ends With the Speaker Tag

Now let's examine a second pattern, in which the sentence ends with the speaker tag: "I think we're going to win the game tonight," said Ben.

Notice the comma and quotation mark placement in this sentence: there is a comma after *tonight*, the last word in the quotation. The quotation mark is placed after that comma. When a sentence ends with a speaker tag, the closing quotation mark is placed after the punctuation that concludes the quote. Students sometimes mistakenly write the equivalent of "I think we're going to win the game tonight", said Ben, and place the comma outside the closing quotation mark. This is an easy mistake to make.

Pattern Three: The Speaker Tag Interrupts the Quotation

Sometimes the speaker tag is in the middle of the sentence, interrupting the quotation, as in the following example: "I think," Ben said, "we're going to win the game tonight."

In this sentence, it's especially important to pay attention to the comma placement. There is a comma inside the quotation mark in the first section of the quote and another comma at the conclusion of the speaker tag (before the second section of the quote begins). One frequent mistake regarding this pattern has to do with capitalization: when a quotation is interrupted by a speaker tag and the sentence has not ended, the second half of the quotation is not capitalized. This is because the sentence isn't over; the author is simply telling the readers who is saying the dialogue.

Pattern Four: There Is No Speaker Tag

Although dialogue is frequently written with speaker tags, this is not always the case. In some instances, readers can determine who is speaking without being explicitly told by the author. In such situations, the author may choose not to directly identify the speaker. This is often the case when an author is describing a conversation. Let's say Ben and one of his teammates are discussing their team's chances of winning that night's game, and the author has firmly established that these are the people involved in the conversation. If it's clear to readers who is speaking, an author may choose not to use a speaker tag, resulting in a sentence such as

> "I think we're going to win the game tonight."

In sentences such as this one, the entire sentence, including all of its punctuation, is enclosed by quotation marks.

Why Commas and Quotation Marks Are Important to Good Dialogue Writing

Commas and quotation marks are important tools for effective writing; if they are not used clearly, readers can't accurately make sense of the dialogue the author is trying to convey. If writers forget to use closing quotation marks in their work, it can be difficult (and sometimes impossible) for readers to tell when the dialogue stops and the narration begins. Similarly, students often mistakenly place speaker tags inside quotation marks, leading to confusion about which parts of the text are actually examples of dialogue. I recently spoke about this topic with a third grade teacher named Julia. She found that her students had difficulty remembering not to put speaker tags inside quotation marks: "My students forget that the part of the sentence that says 'she said' doesn't go in quotes. They put quotes around all of it. It makes their writing hard to follow. I think some of them got lower scores on the state test because of this."

Julia's comments reveal how important it is to help students clearly punctuate dialogue; if they don't, meaning can be lost or muddled. Let's take a look at some examples from children's literature that illustrate how writers use commas and quotation marks when writing dialogue, such as the following example of a speaker tag interrupting a quotation from the book *The SOS File*: "Fred retired last year," Mr. Robinson went on, "but I believe he's still in Atlanta" (Byars, Duffey, & Myers, 2004, p. 45).

In this sentence, the punctuation of the speaker tag is extremely important. If the quotation marks did not close after *year* and reopen before *but*, the sentence would be "Fred retired last year, Mr. Robinson went on, but I believe he's still in Atlanta."

In this changed version of the sentence, readers no longer hear from Mr. Robinson as the authors intended. In the original and correct version of the sentence, the quotation stops before the speaker tag, and resumes again after it, showing readers that Mr. Robinson is the one delivering the dialogue.

As this example demonstrates, correctly punctuating dialogue helps authors clearly express their ideas and eliminates the confusing work Julia noticed her students producing. Writers who clearly use commas and quotation marks when writing dialogue can ensure that their messages are clearly relayed to their readers. Next, we'll look at Ms. Jay's third-grade classroom and see how she uses children's literature to help her students understand how to punctuate dialogue.

A Classroom Snapshot

"Y'all are almost done!" Ms. Jay exclaims. "It's almost time to publish your memoirs!"

Ms. Jay's students began the school year working on memoirs, and they're almost ready for their "publishing party," a class period devoting to reading and celebrating the students' writings. Although she began today's language arts period with such excitement, Ms. Jay had told me during an earlier meeting about something that she was surprised to notice. "A lot of [students] are using dialogue," she said, "but I'm surprised at all the mistakes they're making with quotation marks." Some of the errors Ms. Jay noted were similar to those Julia had observed in her students' work; others were different: "A few students keep forgetting to use quotation marks entirely," Ms. Jay explained, "and some others are using [them] sometimes but not [at] other times. Some more are putting the part of the sentence that tells who's speaking in quotation marks. I need to teach them how to use these quotation marks the right way."

Ms. Jay and I discussed how the quotation marks and commas used to identify dialogue are tools writers use to indicate when a speaker is talking. We agreed that one of the best ways to help the students understand how these tools are used is to show them some examples of published writing and talk about how the authors of those pieces use punctuation to clearly indicate dialogue. We talked about some ways to use published works to help her students understand this concept and apply it to their own writing.

Let's see how Ms. Jay and her students put those ideas into practice in the classroom. The students are on the carpet, and Ms. Jay is standing in front of an easel pad of chart paper, continuing to assert that the students' pieces are almost ready for publication. "But before you do your final edits," she explains, "there's one more thing I want to talk to y'all about." Ms. Jay writes the word *dialogue* on the chart paper next to her and asks the students, "Who can tell me what this means?"

Many of the students raise their hands; the student Ms. Jay calls on states, "It means people talking."

"Rock on!" replies Ms. Jay. "Dialogue refers to the words spoken in a conversation. It can be a conversation between two people or even more than that." Ms. Jay goes on to explain that she is happy that many of the students are using dialogue in their memoirs but that they need to discuss how to punctuate that dialogue. "Punctuating dialogue can be tricky," she says. "There are lots of quotation marks and commas, and it can get confusing."

Ms. Jay continues to explain that the class is going to study the punctuation of dialogue by looking at some published novels and thinking about how those authors punctuated the dialogue in their books. "That will give y'all some good examples to use when you edit your memoirs," she states. "I found some examples of dialogue from a book I really like, called *Stink: The Incredible Shrinking Kid* (Ms. Jay holds up a copy of the book as she says this). We'll look at these examples together and talk about the punctuation."

Ms. Jay turns the page of the large pad of chart paper, revealing a new page with the following text written on it: "While you were gone," said Mrs. Dempster, "we drew a name to see who would get to take Newton home this weekend" (McDonald, 2005, p. 31).

Ms. Jay reads the sentence aloud to the class and explains that Newton is the class's pet newt (this being a class of active third graders, students take this opportunity to ask why *they* don't have a newt as a class pet). She calls the students back to attention and explains that the sentence is important because it's an example of dialogue. "Remember," she cautions, "dialogue can be tough to punctuate because there are so many things happening. What do you notice about the punctuation here?"

"There are quotation marks," responds one student.

"Let's look at those quotation marks," replies Ms. Jay. She explains why the quotation marks stop after the word *gone* and begin again before *we*. "Those are the parts where Mrs. Dempster is actually talking. We put quotation marks only around the things that people say." Ms. Jay then shifts her attention to the commas in the sentence, asking the students what they notice about the commas. One raises her hand and answers, "They're near the quotation marks. There's one after *gone* and one before *we*."

"Rock on! Great!" praises Ms. Jay. "I love how you pointed out that the commas are near the quotation marks. In a sentence like this, in which the quote is interrupted by information about who's talking, there's a comma before the first part of the quote ends and another before the second part of it starts." Students nod while Ms. Jay continues, "If you use a sentence like this one in your memoir, make sure to be careful with your quotation marks. Sometimes it's easy to forget to use them or put the part like 'Mrs. Dempster said' in quotation marks." Ms. Jay hangs the chart paper on the wall so students can refer to it in the future.

"I want y'all to look at another sentence from this book," Ms. Jay tells her students. "It also has dialogue, but it's a little different." She turns the easel pad, revealing the following sentence from *Shrink: The Incredible Shrinking Kid*: "You have all the luck," said Webster (p. 31). Ms. Jay explains that the class will think about how this sentence is similar to and different from the previous one: "There are some ways this sentence is like the other one and some ways it's different. What do you notice?"

"The 'said' part is at the end," answers one student.

"Rock on!" responds Ms. Jay. "The speaker tag, or the part that says who said it, is at the end here, not in the middle. What do you notice about the quotation marks here?"

Another student states, "They start before *you* and end after *luck*."

"I love it!" responds Ms. Jay. "The quotation marks start and end after those words because that's what Webster said. I also want you to notice the comma here. It comes right after the word *end*, but it's still inside the quotation mark. That part's tricky, but try to remember that quotation marks go outside the commas in sentences like that."

Ms. Jay transitions to the next activity: "Now, I have one more job for you. I've rewritten this sentence so that the speaker tag comes first. I want you to help me put the right punctuation on it." Ms. Jay turns to another piece of chart paper with the following text written on it: Webster said You have all the luck. "Other than the period at the end," she explains, "this sentence doesn't have any punctuation. Let's put that punctuation in it together." She asks students to share their ideas and facilitates discussion as the comments roll in. After several responses, the class has a correctly punctuated sentence: Webster said, "You have all the luck."

To close, Ms. Jay calls the students' attention to the comma after *said* and then turns the focus to the students' writings: "Remember to include that comma after the speaker tag. It's easy to forget, but it helps readers know a quotation is coming. Y'all did a great job on these sentences. Now I want you to look at your memoir drafts and check the punctuation of your quotations. All these sentences we just looked at will be posted on the wall so you can check them out. I'll be coming around and talking with you while we do this. I'm passing back your writing folders now. Once you get yours, start looking at your memoir."

Recommendations for Teaching Students How to Use Commas and Quotation Marks When Writing Dialogue

In this section, I describe a step-by-step instructional process for helping students understand how to use commas and quotation marks when writing dialogue.

1. Show students examples of comma and quotation mark use in published texts.
2. Discuss the published texts with students.
3. Ask students to provide punctuation for unpunctuated examples.
4. Have students edit their own work with this concept in mind.

These steps were designed to help students think carefully about why commas and quotation marks are important to clear and effective dialogue writing. The use of published texts as models and tools for analysis helps students understand how to punctuate dialogue and allows them to apply this knowledge to their own writing.

1. Show students examples of comma and quotation mark use in published texts.

To get students started thinking about this concept, show them examples of comma and quotation mark use in published texts. Providing these models gives students concrete examples to use when wrestling with this concept. Instead of talking about comma and quotation mark use in the abstract, looking at the ways published writers use commas and quotation marks shows students that this is something that writers incorporate into their craft. In addition, using examples from texts students enjoy can enhance student engagement, increasing their participation in the activity. One teacher I spoke with about this instructional method told me that her students didn't have much interest in talking about punctuation at first but began to when they noticed that the lesson incorporated examples from books they enjoyed. Because almost all books (except for plays) contain examples of dialogue punctuated with commas and quotation marks, finding texts that are at students' reading levels and appeal to their interests is easy.

2. Discuss the published texts with students.

After showing students examples, I recommend talking with them about why the authors of those texts punctuate dialogue using commas and quotation marks. Two key points to address in these conversations are (1) quotation marks are important because they indicate the exact words someone said, and (2) commas in dialogue are important because they frequently mark when quotations are starting or ending. For example, consider the following sentence Ms. Jay shared with her class: "While you were gone," said Mrs. Dempster, "we drew a name to see who would get to take Newton home this weekend" (McDonald, 2005, p. 31). In this sentence, the quotation marks clearly separate what Mrs. Dempster said from what she didn't, and the commas mark the transitions from the first part of the quotation to the speaker tag and then back from the speaker tag to the second part of the quotation.

A central concept to drive home during these discussions is that writers put only the exact words someone said in quotation marks. Although this is a concept that students usually know in theory, they sometimes make mistakes related to it when writing dialogue. To clearly illustrate this for students, I show them a correct version of a sentence and then a version of the sentence with the speaker tag incorrectly included in quotation marks. As part of this discussion, we talk about why the second version is incorrect. The figures below illustrate a sentence I've used to explain this. The first version (Figure 3.1, page 32) contains a sentence from *Nate the Great on the Owl Express*: "Miss Olivia took care of everything," Willie said (Sharmat & Sharmat, 2004, p.15).

The second (Figure 3.2, page 32) contains the same sentence, except it is rewritten so the speaker tag is included in quotation marks. In the first version, readers hear directly from Willie that Miss Olivia took care of everything. Willie is definitely the speaker in this sentence. The second (incorrect) version is more confusing because *Willie said* is also included in the quotation marks. The proper use of quotation marks is important to the clarity of this sentence.

3. Ask students to provide punctuation for unpunctuated examples.

Once you've shown students examples from published texts and discussed the punctuation in those examples, I recommend asking students to provide punctuation for some unpunctuated sentences you provide. Choose an example of dialogue from a text, and write it on the board or a large piece of paper without any commas or quotation marks. Ask students to punctuate it based on what they've learned about commas and quotation

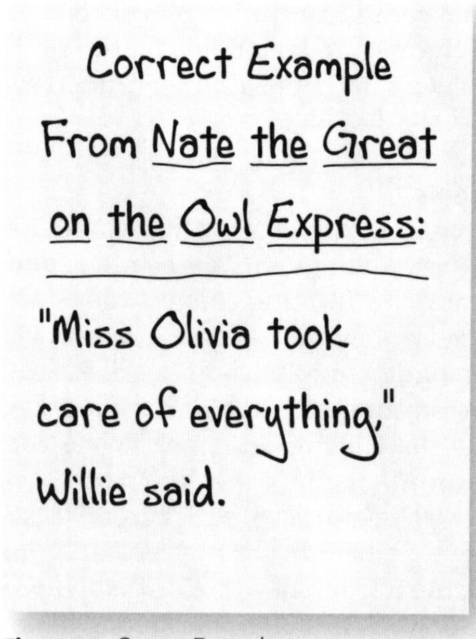

Correct Example

From <u>Nate</u> <u>the</u> <u>Great</u>
<u>on</u> <u>the</u> <u>Owl</u> Express:

"Miss Olivia took
care of everything,"
Willie said.

Figure 3.1 Correct Example

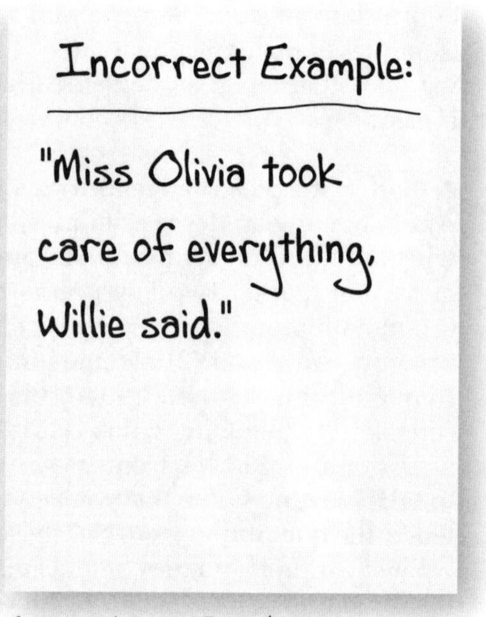

Incorrect Example:

"Miss Olivia took
care of everything,
Willie said."

Figure 3.2 Incorrect Example

marks. There are a number of ways to do this: in a whole class discussion, as Ms. Jay did; as a small group activity; or as individual work. I like to do this one time as a whole class and then another time in small groups. When the students work in small groups, I closely monitor how well they are grasping the concept. If I notice any high-frequency mistakes during this activity, I address those topics before moving forward.

4. Have students edit their own work with this concept in mind.

Once you're comfortable with your students' understandings of commas and quotation marks, have them edit their own works with this concept in mind. Ask students to look at the dialogue in the pieces they're currently writing, make sure commas and quotation marks are properly used, and make any necessary changes. This application provides a sense of completion to the lesson—students have moved from looking at these forms of punctuation in published works to discussing them to applying their knowledge to their own writing.

This is also a good time to hold individual writing conferences with students and focus specifically on this issue. Short, focused conferences can prevent students from getting overwhelmed and make sure they leave the conference with a deeper understanding of the lesson's focal concept. Ralph Fletcher and Joann Portalupi (2001) encourage teachers to teach one particular skill or strategy during writing conferences; focusing specifically on punctuating dialogue can help students master this concept so they can apply it to their future work.

Final Thoughts on Using Commas and Quotation Marks When Writing Dialogue

The information below summarizes major points from this chapter, including what this grammatical concept is, why it's important for good writing, and how one might teach it for maximum effectiveness.

- ◆ Using commas and quotation marks when writing dialogue is included in Common Core Language Standard 3.2.
- ◆ Authors use four typical sentence patterns when writing dialogue:
  - The speaker tag interrupts the quotation.
  - The sentence ends with the speaker tag.
  - The sentence begins with a speaker tag.
  - There is no speaker tag.
- ◆ Quotation marks are important because they indicate the exact words someone said.
- ◆ Commas in dialogue are important because they frequently mark when quotations are starting or ending.
- ◆ Students' mistakes with quotation marks can lead to confusing writing in which the identity of the speaker is unclear.
- ◆ When teaching students about using commas and quotation marks in dialogue, try these four things:
  - Show students examples of published texts that use these forms of punctuation.
  - Discuss the published texts with student.
  - Ask students to provide punctuation for unpunctuated examples.
  - Have students edit their own work with this concept in mind.

4

Simple, Compound, and Complex Sentences

What Are Simple, Compound, and Complex Sentences?

Common Core Language Standard 3.1 calls for students to "produce simple, compound, and complex sentences" (Common Core Standards, 2010) as part of a broader standard that requires students to demonstrate command of grammatical conventions. These three sentence types provide variation in writing, as they differ in their structures, effects, and amounts of detail. To understand the differences among these three sentence types, it's important to grasp a fundamental concept: the *independent clause*. An independent clause is a group of words that contains a subject and a verb and expresses a complete thought. For example, "The lions rested" is an independent clause; *lions* is the subject and *rested* is the verb. The independent clause is the starting point for thinking about the differences among simple, compound, and complex sentences because all three sentence types contain at least one independent clause—the differences lie in what else the sentences contain. Let's explore each sentence type in more detail.

Simple Sentences

A simple sentence is made up of one independent clause. The example above—"The lions rested"—is an example of a simple sentence. Simple sentences are basic building blocks of writing; there are times when writers want to create longer sentences that string together multiple ideas and include additional details, but there are also instances when writers may want to express an idea in a simple sentence.

Compound Sentences

A compound sentence contains two or more independent clauses joined by a coordinator. Let's turn our earlier example into a compound sentence. Instead of "The lions rested," we could write, "The lions rested, so most of the jungle was quiet." In this sentence, "The lions rested" is one independent clause, and "most of the jungle was quiet" is another. The combination of these independent clauses in one sentence makes it a compound sentence. As discussed in more detail below, the coordinating conjunction *so* joins the two independent clauses.

When discussing compound sentences with students, addressing how the independent clauses are linked is important. There are two ways to link independent clauses in compound sentences: (1) with coordinating conjunctions, and (2) with semicolons.

Coordinating conjunctions. Some especially common coordinating conjunctions are *for*, *and*, *nor*, *but*, *or*, *yet*, and *so*. Jeff Anderson (2005) used the pneumonic *FANBOYS* to help his students remember these coordinating conjunctions—each letter of the word *FANBOYS* refers to one of the coordinating conjunctions. These conjunctions (used with commas) link the independent clauses in compound sentences and allow writers to combine multiple thoughts in a single sentence. In the compound sentence example about resting lions, *so* is the coordinating conjunction that links the independent clauses: "The lions rested, *so* most of the jungle was quiet." It's important to note that a comma precedes *so*; coordinating conjunctions that link independent clauses are accompanied by commas. However, coordinating conjunctions are not the only ways to link independent clauses in compound sentences.

Semicolons. Like coordinating conjunctions, semicolons also link independent clauses in compound sentences. Writers sometimes choose to use semicolons instead of coordinating conjunctions because semicolons can be more concise and direct. Instead of linking two independent clauses using one of the coordinating conjunctions, a semicolon allows the independent clauses to simply be next to each other. In the example about resting lions, replacing *so* with a semicolon yields "The lions rested; most of the jungle was quiet."

Complex Sentences

Although compound sentences can contain multiple independent clauses, complex sentences contain both independent and dependent clauses. Understanding this kind of sentence requires understanding what a dependent clause is. An independent clause contains a subject and a verb and expresses a complete thought. A dependent clause also contains a subject and a verb, but it can't stand on its own and doesn't express a complete thought. Let's use the lion example again to illustrate this concept.

We already examined an example of a simple sentence: "The lions rested." In addition, we looked at two examples of compound sentences:

"The lions rested, so most of the jungle was quiet" and "The lions rested; most of the jungle was quiet." Now we see a similar sentence as a complex sentence: "Because the lions rested, most of the jungle was quiet." What makes this a complex sentence? It contains two clauses ("Because the lions rested" and "most of the jungle was quiet"), but these are not independent clauses linked by either a coordinating conjunction or semicolon, as the clauses in compound sentences are. One clause *cannot* stand on its own as a sentence ("Because the lions rested"); the other one *can* ("most of the jungle was quiet"). The word *because* turns the opening clause in this sentence into a dependent clause because it makes it impossible for the opening clause to stand on its own. Some other high-frequency words that begin dependent clauses are *because, before, while, although, if, until, when, which, who,* and *after*.

Figures 4.1, 4.2, and 4.3 (page 38) illustrate some key points related to simple, compound, and complex sentences.

Why Simple, Compound, and Complex Sentences Are Important to Good Writing

Part of helping students produce simple, compound, and complex sentences is helping students understand *why* writers use these kinds of sentences. When students understand that each sentence type is important to good writing, they will ultimately be able to apply this knowledge to their own work. Simple, compound, and complex sentences are important because of the variety they can add to writing. Each sentence type is a tool writers can use to shape their work in specific ways. Authors choose their sentence types intentionally: a simple sentence might be used to make a particular point, a compound sentence might combine two points, and a complex sentence may use a dependent clause to provide contextual information about why or how something took place.

To further illustrate how and why writers use simple, compound, and complex sentences, let's examine how E.B. White used them in his classic novel *Charlotte's Web*. It features a range of sentence types, making it useful for demonstrating why writers use certain sentences for particular effects. To get started, let's look at a simple sentence from this novel: "The barn was very large" (White, 1952, p. 13). This sentence consists of one independent clause and allows the author to make a specific point. If White had wanted to, he certainly could have added a dependent clause to provide more detail or combined this independent clause with another to link those ideas. However, White chose to deliver this sentence concisely and directly, providing readers with this information in a simple sentence.

At other times in *Charlotte's Web*, White chose to use compound sentences to provide information. When describing how busy the Zuckerman family had grown while entertaining visitors, White used a compound sentence to provide insight into how the presence of those visitors impacted the family's everyday life: "The blackberries got ripe, and Mrs. Zuckerman

Figure 4.1 Simple Sentence

Grammatical Concept	Simple Sentence
What is a simple sentence?	A simple sentence is made up of one independent clause.
What is an example of a simple sentence?	"The lions rested."
Why is this an example of a simple sentence?	It contains one independent clause and no additional clauses of any kind.

Figure 4.2 Compound Sentence

Grammatical Concept	Compound Sentence
What is a compound sentence?	A compound sentence is made up of two or more independent clauses joined by a coordinator— a comma and a coordinating conjunction or a semicolon.
What are some examples of compound sentences?	1. "The lions rested, so most of the jungle was quiet." 2. "The lions rested; most of the jungle was quiet."
Why are these examples of compound sentences?	• Each sentence contains two independent clauses. • In example 1, two independent clauses are joined by a comma and the coordinating conjunction *so*. • In example 2, two independent clauses are joined by a semicolon.

Figure 4.3 Complex Sentence

Grammatical Concept	Complex Sentence
What is a complex sentence?	A complex sentence is made up of one independent clause and at least one dependent clause.
What is an example of a complex sentence?	"Because the lions rested, most of the jungle was quiet."
Why is this an example of a complex sentence?	• It contains a dependent and an independent clause. • "Because the lions rested" is a dependent clause (it cannot stand on its own), and "most of the jungle was quiet" is an independent clause (it can stand on its own as a sentence).

failed to put up any blackberry jam" (p. 84). This sentence links two related independent clauses with the coordinating conjunction *and*. Although White could have written these independent clauses as separate sentences, linking them to form a compound sentence impacts the writing in two major ways: (1) It eliminates the short, choppy sentences that would be present if the sentence had been divided, and (2) it illustrates the connection between these events, making sure readers understand that it was unusual for Mrs. Zuckerman to fail to make blackberry jam when those berries ripened. White's purposeful use of this compound sentence allowed him to make his point.

White also included complex sentences in *Charlotte's Web*, using the information in a dependent clause to provide contextual details related to an independent clause, such as in this sentence: "While the rat and the spider and the little girl watched, Wilbur climbed again to the top of the manure pile, full of energy and hope" (p. 58). In this sentence, "While the rat and spider and the little girl watched" is a dependent clause. Although it cannot stand alone, it still provides useful information. Without this clause, readers wouldn't know about the rat, spider, and little girl watching Wilbur. This information lets readers know that others are watching Wilbur and creates a different situation than if he were climbing the pile alone. In this scene, Wilbur climbs to the top of the pile so he can attempt to spin a web. The presence of an audience contributes to Wilbur's behavior; he later admits to Charlotte he was "just trying to show off" (p. 60).

Why are simple, compound, and complex sentences important to good writing? These sentence types are tools writers can use for specific purposes. There isn't one version that authors should always use; it all depends on an author's objective for a particular sentence. As White showed in *Charlotte's Web*, there are certain situations in which each type is the preferred option. When talking with students about simple, compound, and complex sentences, teachers can emphasize the uses of the different kinds of sentences and present them as tools that students can apply to their writing. By describing these sentences as context-specific, teachers can encourage students to think carefully about *why* writers make certain choices. Let's look inside Ms. Jay's third-grade classroom and see how she helps her students think carefully about using each of these sentence types.

A Classroom Snapshot

Autumn is now in full force in the town where Ms. Jay and her third graders live. The changing leaves and cooler temperatures bring with them both accomplishments and new challenges. On the accomplishments side, Ms. Jay's students did a wonderful job on the memoirs they started at the beginning of the school year. Thus far, they've made great progress with pronoun reference, subject-verb agreement, and the use of quotation marks and commas to indicate dialogue in their writing. Though

Ms. Jay is pleased with her students' work so far, she knows there are many additional concepts to teach.

These concepts, in her mind, are necessitated by both the Common Core Standards and her students' writing. "They're doing great," she says of her students' progress, "but there are a lot more standards to cover and a lot more ways to help them become better writers." Ms. Jay's comment reveals not only her awareness of the Common Core Standards requirements but also the connection between students learning grammatical concepts and applying them to their writing. The link between grammar and writing instruction is present in today's lesson: Ms. Jay and her students are talking about how and why writers use simple, compound, and complex sentences. In the previous class, Ms. Jay went over the differences among these concepts. She showed students examples of each kind and talked with them about independent clauses, dependent clauses, and coordinating conjunctions. Pieces of chart paper defining these concepts still hang on the room's walls; Ms. Jay left them up intentionally so she can refer to them during today's class. Because the students have already discussed the basics of these sentences, the objective of today's lesson is to help students understand *why* writers use each of the sentence types. Ms. Jay hopes to help students think metacognitively about the uses of simple, compound, and complex sentences. "I want them to understand that these are different kinds of sentences they can use in their writing for different reasons," she explains. "I think looking at how [these sentence types] are used in literature can help with this."

Ms. Jay and I wrap up our conversation, and the students enter the room. Today they are coming from art class, and many still have paint and marker on them as they converge on the class rug. "Great job entering the room and finding your spots," remarks Ms. Jay. "From the markings on you, it looks like y'all had fun in art." The students laugh briefly; Ms. Jay pauses and then introduces the day's lesson. "Yesterday, we talked about simple, compound, and complex sentences. Let's go over them." Ms. Jay directs students to the hanging pieces of chart paper that define these sentence types and show examples of them. After she reviews the concepts and asks students to explain some key differences among them, Ms. Jay directs students toward the day's focus, explaining that she's going to use some examples from the book *The Twits*, which she has been reading aloud to the class, to show the students how a writer uses each sentence type. "Here's an example of a simple sentence," she states. She places the book on the document projector so all the students can see it and points to the sentence: "Mrs. Twit was no better than her husband" (Dahl, 1980, p. 8). "This sentence has one independent clause," she explains. "It doesn't have any dependent clauses and isn't linked with another independent clause. That makes it a simple sentence."

Next, Ms. Jay asks the students to consider why the author used a simple sentence in this situation. "The sentence says one thing," explains one student. Ms. Jay builds off this response: "Rock on! Good stuff, man.

This sentence says one thing. It makes one point. If it was a compound or a complex sentence, it would give more information, but the author wants to make just one point here: that Mrs. Twit was no better than her husband."

Ms. Jay states that she will next show the class an example of a compound sentence and asks, "Can someone remind us what a compound sentence is?" A student raises her hand and volunteers her thoughts: "It has two independent clauses."

"Yes! Two independent clauses in one sentence," responds Ms. Jay. "They can be combined by a semicolon or a coordinating conjunction," she explains, directing the class's attention to the chart paper on the wall that explains the features of compound sentences. "Here's a compound sentence from *The Twits*." She opens the book to a new page, places it on the document projector, and points to the sentence: "He went on drinking his beer, and his evil mind kept working away on the latest horrid trick he was going to play on the old woman" (Dahl, 1980, p.11). Ms. Jay reads the sentence aloud and then explains, "This is a compound sentence because it has two independent clauses. Those clauses are linked by a coordinating conjunction." As she says this, she points to the coordinating conjunction *and*.

Ms. Jay asks the students why the author used a compound sentence here instead of using two simple sentences. Students look around, unsure, when one blurts out, "To combine them."

"Rock on! To combine them!" responds Ms. Jay. "The author might want to combine these independent clauses. Why do you think that might be?"

The student replies, "Maybe because they're related. They're both about things that the guy was doing."

"Yes!" responds Ms. Jay. "They're both about Mr. Twit. An author might combine two independent clauses to show that they're related. An author might do this to avoid having two short, choppy sentences when a longer one would sound better."

Next, Ms. Jay transitions to the final sentence type, telling the students she will now show them an example of a complex sentence. She opens her book to a new page, places it on the document projector, and directs the students' attention to the sentence: "Because of all this, Mr. Twit never went really hungry" (Dahl, 1980, p.7). "Here's another sentence about Mr. Twit," she explains. "The first part, which says 'Because of all this,' is a dependent clause. It can't stand on its own as a sentence. The second part, 'Mr. Twit never went really hungry,' is an independent clause. It has a subject and a verb, and it can stand on its own. Remember from when we read this part that this section is about how Mr. Twit can keep food in his beard?" Students nod, some laughing at Mr. Twit's keeping food in his beard. "That's what the word *because* at the beginning is referring to."

Ms. Jay then asks the students, "Why, do you think, did the author use a complex sentence here?" A student raises her hand and shares: "Because the first part explains why he never got hungry."

"Yes!"!" exclaims Ms. Jay. "The dependent clause in this sentence, 'Because of all this,' explains why Mr. Twit never really went hungry. This part of the sentence is important because of the information it provides. Most complex sentences are like this: the dependent clauses provide some extra detail." Ms. Jay concludes the lesson by telling the students that, in the next class, they'll look through books from the classroom library and pick out simple, compound, and complex sentences. "Once you find them," she explains, "you'll explain why the author might have used that sentence type, as we did today."

Recommendations for Teaching Simple, Compound, and Complex Sentences

In this section, I describe a step-by-step instructional process to use when working with students on simple, compound, and complex sentences:

1. Discuss the strengths of each sentence type.
2. Ask students to identify examples of these sentences in their independent reading books.
3. Have students analyze the benefits of the examples they found.
4. Have students purposefully use these sentence types in their own writing.

These steps were designed to help students think about why writers use simple, compound, and complex sentences and to help students reflect on how each concept can be strategically used to enhance a piece of writing. Because these recommendations are intended to be applications of the students' knowledge of simple, compound, and complex sentences, it's important to provide students with a basic overview of these concepts using the information and examples in the beginning of this chapter before beginning the steps described.

1. Discuss the strengths of each sentence type.
Talking with students about the strengths of each sentence type is a fundamental step in helping them think critically about why writers use simple, compound, and complex sentences. To strategically use these sentence types in their writing, students need to understand why a writer might use one instead of another. A major strength of Ms. Jay's lesson was her emphasis on why the author of *The Twits* may have chosen to use a simple sentence in one situation, a compound sentence in another situation, and a complex sentence in another. Her discussion of this topic gave her students a strong introduction into the purposeful use of these sentences.

To help students understand the strengths of each sentence type, I recommend conducting specific, focused mini-lessons that highlight the

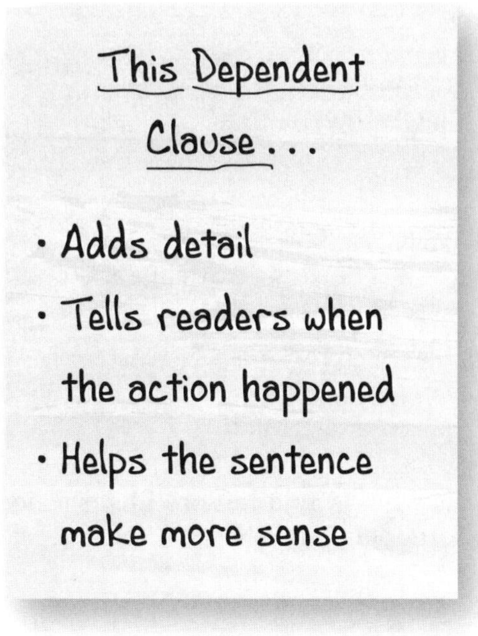

Figure 4.4 Benefits of Dependent Clauses

This Dependent

Clause . . .

- Adds detail
- Tells readers when the action happened
- Helps the sentence make more sense

benefits of using simple, compound, and complex sentences. In a recent visit to a third-grade class, I conducted one of these mini-lessons, leading the students in a conversation about the benefits of complex sentences. I used the following text from *Voyage to the Volcano*, a Magic School Bus chapter book: "When Jim heard our big yellow copter, he looked up and waved" (Stamper, 2003, p. 49). I discussed with students some reasons the author may have used a dependent clause—"When Jim heard the big yellow copter." As a concluding activity, I wrote down the students' thoughts on the benefits of using this dependent clause. (See Figure 4.4, above.)

These responses show the students' understanding of how the dependent clause enhances this sentence and therefore the benefits of using a complex sentence in this situation. Without the dependent clause, this sentence would contain very little context or detail. With it, the sentence shows a relationship between two events and tells readers when an important action took place.

2. Ask students to identify examples of these sentences in their independent reading books.

After talking with students about the benefits of using simple, compound, and complex sentences in various situations, I recommend asking students to look through the books they're reading and find examples of each sentence type. Whether students are reading one text as a class or different texts based on their individual levels, having them find examples of simple, compound, and complex sentences in published texts increases

Figure 4.5 Model of Sentence Analysis Chart

Sentence	Sentence Type	Rewritten as a Different Type	Benefit of Writing the Sentence the Way It Was Originally Written
"When Jim heard our big yellow copter, he looked up and waved."	Complex	"Jim heard our big yellow copter. He looked up and waved." (Rewritten as two simple sentences).	The original writing links the clauses together and shows when the action happened.

A blank version of this table, to copy and use with your students, is included as a supplemental download (see page iv).

their familiarity with these sentence types. In addition, this practice further affirms that these sentences are tools published authors use in their writing.

3. Have students analyze the benefits of the examples they found.

Once students have found examples of these sentence types in the books they're reading, ask them to analyze the benefits of the examples they found. Doing this requires students to think about why the author might have used these sentence types. Engaging in such reflection improves students' metacognition of these concepts by further helping them think of these sentence types as tools writers purposefully implement. This activity builds on the whole-class discussion described in step one of this section—the main difference is that, in this step, students conduct the analysis on their own. Teachers will want to check in with students and support them, but it's important to ask students to analyze these texts using their own skills and ideas.

To facilitate student analysis, I like to provide them with the chart depicted in Figure 4.5 (above). This chart asks students to identify the type of sentence, explain how it would be different if it were written as another type, and describe a benefit of writing it in the way it was written. Figure 4.5 shows how I modeled this activity with the sentence from *Voyage to the Volcano* previously described in this section. A blank version of this chart is available as a supplemental download (see page iv).

4. Ask students to purposefully use these sentence types in their own writing.

Because one goal of this method of grammar instruction is to help students apply their understandings of grammatical concepts to their own writing, the final step of this instructional recommendation is to ask students to use each sentence type in their own work. Putting these concepts into practice helps students continue to realize the benefits of thinking strategically about simple, compound, and complex sentences. When doing an activity like this, I ask students why thinking carefully about which sentence type to use in a particular situation might be important. One student responded to this question by explaining, "There are times you'll want to use each of these sentences. It just depends on how the sentence goes along with what you want to say." To help students think critically about using simple, compound, and complex sentences (as this student did), I meet with them in one-on-one writing conferences in which they show me at least one example of each sentence type and talk to me about why they chose to use that sentence type in that specific situation. These conversations help me understand the students' thought processes and see how they're purposefully using each sentence type in their writing.

Final Thoughts on Simple, Compound, and Complex Sentences

The following information summarizes major points from this chapter, including what this grammatical concept is, why it's important for good writing, and how one might teach it for maximum effectiveness.

- ◆ Simple, compound, and complex sentences are included in Common Core Language Standard 3.1.
  - A simple sentence contains one independent clause (a group of words, with a subject and verb, that expresses a complete thought).
  - A compound sentence contains two or more independent clauses joined by a semicolon or a coordinating conjunction.
  - A complex sentence contains an independent clause and at least one dependent clause.
- ◆ Writers use each sentence type purposefully, based on the kind of information they need to express and how they want to express it.
- ◆ When teaching simple, compound, and complex sentences, try these four things:
  - Describe the strengths of each.
  - Ask students to find examples in the books they're reading.
  - Have students analyze these examples.
  - Ask students to purposefully include each sentence type in their own writing.

5

Recognizing Differences Between Spoken and Written Standard English

What Does "Recognize the Differences Between Spoken and Written Standard English" Mean?

Common Core Language Standard 3.3 calls for students to "Recognize and observe differences between the conventions of spoken and written standard English" as part of a more general statement that students should "Use knowledge of language and its conventions when writing, speaking, reading, or listening" (Common Core, 2010). In this chapter, we'll look at the differences between spoken and written standard English and consider how to help students understand these differences and apply this understanding to their writing.

Robert MacNeil and William Cran's book *Do You Speak American?* (2005) highlights distinctions between the different ways English is typically spoken and written. These authors explain that, although spoken English is often informal and not standardized, written English generally conforms to the expectations of standard English. To further understand the differences between spoken and written English, it's helpful to think about the ideas of *audience, purpose,* and *language expectation*. All communication has a particular audience in mind and varies in certain ways based on that audience. For example, students may use certain expressions and slang terms with their friends that they would not use with teachers and other adults. However, audience does not completely control the style of communication; purpose also plays a major role in how one communicates. When recently working with a third-grade class, I listened to a teacher talk with a student about the basketball jersey the student was wearing. They talked about the student's favorite teams and players and how long he had played basketball. In this conversation, the student had a much more casual tone than the persuasive essay he turned in during that day's language arts period. The basketball conversation included expressions and some basketball-specific jargon; the persuasive essay was much more formal and observed more of the conventions of standard English. Though the audience was the same in each instance, the purpose of each was different, resulting in a different style of communication.

As this example shows, the combination of audience and purpose affects the language expectation associated with the communication. This "equation" can be used to help students understand the differences between spoken and written standard English. Spoken English is often more informal because the audience and purpose do not require formal communication. Written English, however, needs a more formal tone when required by the audience and purpose. There are times when written English is not especially formal, such as in a note or text message. Similarly, there are times when spoken English is rather formal, such as in a speech or class presentation. Because of this, considering the audience and purpose when determining the expectations of a particular situation is especially important. As this chapter continues, we'll look at some even more specific ways of bringing the ideas of audience, purpose, and language expectations into the classroom to help students write effectively.

Why Recognizing Differences Between Spoken and Written Standard English Is Important to Good Writing

Recognizing the differences in the conventions of spoken and written standard English is an important tool for students to master and be able to apply to their own work. If they grasp this concept, they can communicate appropriately in a range of situations, using the language each context calls for. Writers who can think critically about audience, purpose, and expectations can craft messages that communicate with readers in the styles they expect. You would be surprised if you looked up an encyclopedia entry on a historical figure to find it written in casual, conversational language—for example, the statement "John F. Kennedy was awesome!" does not provide the kind of information an encyclopedia reader would expect. Figure 5.1 (page 49) addresses why audience, purpose, and language expectations are each important to effective communication.

As Figure 5.1 illustrates, considering with whom writers are communicating and the reason for that communication is important when making choices about the kind of language to use. Generally, spoken English is characterized by an informal, conversational style, and written standard English represents "textbook" language in which grammatical rules and customs are followed. As the classroom snapshot section illustrates, there are times when students might know the rules of grammar but not understand that certain situations call for writers to adhere to the expectations of written standard English. Because of this, it's important to teach students

Figure 5.1 Why Audience, Purpose, and Language Expectation Are Important

Component of Communication	What It Is	Why Understanding It Is Important to Effective Communication
Audience	The person or group of people with which you will be communicating	Understanding your audience allows you to deliver your message in a specific way geared toward its interests and characteristics.
Purpose	The reason you are communicating with your audience. This includes the kinds of information you plan to provide and whether you intend to entertain, inform, or persuade.	Understanding your purpose helps you determine which information you are going to share and the style in which you are going to share it.
Language Expectation	The result of combining audience and purpose, this is the way your audience anticipates how you will communicate with it and the style of language you will use.	Understanding language expectations will help you determine whether to use standard English or a less formal language style.

to distinguish between situations that require the conventions of standard English and those in which informal English is acceptable. Don't assume that students will know to use standard English when they write unless they understand the meaning behind this concept.

A Classroom Snapshot

Ms. Jay and her students are firmly entrenched in writing reports about habitats. The class has been researching habitats such as grasslands, deserts, tropical rain forests, temperate forests, and tundras and the animals and plants that live in those places. The students have brainstormed topics, discussed research strategies, and learned about considering the trustworthiness of different sources. However, in today's class, Ms. Jay is leading a mini-lesson unlike any others she has covered in this unit: writing in standard English.

When we met prior to this class, Ms. Jay shared with me the one aspect of the students' work that surprised her: the style of language used so far in the students' reports. The language wasn't inappropriate or objectionable, but it was unlike what she expected to see in informational reports. "One thing about their first drafts really surprised me. The language in many of them is just really casual, like talking to a friend." Ms. Jay continued to explain, "I've noticed a lot of words like *wow* and phrases like 'This thing about tundras is cool.' I like that they're excited, but that's not the way a report should sound. [The reports] really just sound as though students are talking, not writing." As Ms. Jay and I continued to talk, it became clear that the problem was not that the students didn't *know* standard English; the problem was that they didn't understand this situation called for them to *use* standard English and didn't know how to determine which contexts called for which levels of formality. We talked about some ways to help the students understand the language expectations for this assignment and planned a lesson based on those ideas.

Let's transition back to Ms. Jay's lesson and see how she helps her students understand the idea of language expectations. She assembles the students on the carpet and compliments them on the research they've done so far on their reports. "Y'all have found so many *great* pieces of information on your habitats! I'm really proud of the research you've done. Rock on!" Students smile, and she continues, "But today I'm going to ask you to think about something a little different. Someone tell me an example of an animal that lives in your habitat."

Students call out, and animal names fill the air. Ms. Jay writes them on the easel pad: grizzly bear, shark, polar bear, penguin, monkey, lion. After she finishes recording these names, Ms. Jay steps back and looks at the list. "Yes!! There are some great animals here. Love it! If you were going to tell one of your friends in our class about one of these animals, what do you think you'd say?"

One student raises his hand and states, "I'd say that sharks have really sharp teeth and are scary."

"Rock on!" exclaims Ms. Jay. Next to the word *shark*, she writes "Has really sharp teeth and is scary."

"Anyone else?" she asks.

Another student shares: "I think penguins are really cute." The class laughs. "I would tell my friend that penguins live in cold weather and are really cute."

"Fabulous!" Ms. Jay says. Next to *penguin* on the easel pad, she writes, "Lives in cold weather and is really cute."

"Here, I'll give you another example of an animal. Two days ago, I saw a mouse in my living room," explains Ms. Jay. "I was so scared. I called my best friend afterward, and I said, 'The mouse was tiny, but I didn't care. I was still soooo scared!' If I were writing a report on mice, is that how I'd write it? Tiny but sooooo scary?" Students shake their heads.

"When we write," explains Ms. Jay, "and especially when we write factual papers, such as reports, we want to use standard English. Standard

English is English that follows the rules of writing. Sometimes when we talk, we say things that don't really follow the rules, because a lot of times having a conversation is more casual. When you have a conversation, you might use casual words or expressions. If you write in your report, 'Hey, check out this stuff about rain forests,' you're being casual and writing as though you're having a conversation. If you say 'The rain forest is home to many different kinds of animals,' you're using standard English. Can you see the difference?"

Students nod. Ms. Jay turns to a blank page on the easel pad and writes these examples:

Conversational English:	"Hey, check out this stuff about rain forests."
Standard English:	"The rain forest is home to many different kinds of animals."

Ms. Jay explains to the students that they will be going to the media center to look up information about the habitats they are researching. She says that they can look at books on their topic and use the computers to access encyclopedia entries. They have already been to the media center as part of this project to check out books and look up information, but the purpose of this visit is a bit different. "Look up some materials and find things you can use in your reports, but I also want you to pay attention to the language used in the things you find," she explains. "When we come back, I'll ask you if it's standard or conversational English. Now go for it!"

The students and Ms. Jay proceed to the media center, where they look up materials on the habitats they are studying. As the students comb through this information, Ms. Jay comes around and checks in with them. I listen to some conversations and notice that she is directing their attention to the kind of language used in the text, helping them realize that these resources utilize standard English. After this continues for about 20 minutes, Ms. Jay brings the students back to the classroom and debriefs.

"I can't wait to hear your ideas! What did you notice about the language?" she asks. "Standard or conversational?" Several students raise their hands and reply that the materials they studied were written in standard English. Ms. Jay follows up by asking the students how they could tell, to which a student replies, "The encyclopedia I read doesn't use expressions or other things like that. It doesn't sound like how you'd talk to your friends."

"Rock on! Great description," responds Ms. Jay. "There are times when you'll use conversational English, as when you talk to your friends, but this report is a time to use standard English. Tomorrow, I'm going to hand you the drafts of your reports, and we're going to work on changing the conversational English some of you are using in your reports to standard English. I'll conference with you and talk to you about it some more."

Later that week, Ms. Jay informed me that the students were making great progress changing the conversational language in their reports into standard English. "The best part," she explained, "is now they think about this on their own. I was conferencing with [a student], and she pointed out that something needed to be in standard English before I even noticed it."

Recommendations for Teaching Students to Recognize the Differences Between Spoken and Written Standard English

In this section, I describe a step-by-step instructional process to use when teaching students to recognize the differences between spoken and written standard English:

1. Activate students' prior knowledge about spoken English.
2. Have students look at examples of written standard English.
3. Work with students to compare the features and uses of spoken English and written English.
4. Help students apply their knowledge of these differences to their own writing.

These steps were designed to help students understand the differences between spoken and written standard English, determine when to use each, and ultimately use their knowledge to enhance their own works.

1. Activate students' prior knowledge about spoken English.

Students have a great deal of prior knowledge about spoken English; after all, they have been speaking it for most of their lives and in a variety of contexts. Though teachers don't need to teach them *how* to engage in spoken, conversational English, teachers do need to tap into what students already know and use that knowledge to best teach them. Ms. Jay did this in her lesson when she asked the students to consider how they would describe an animal to a friend. Their responses provided examples of conversational English that she could then compare with the conventions of written standard English. There are many ways to activate what students already know about this concept. Two examples are (1) have students record a conversation with a friend and listen to the kinds of words used in the conversation, and (2) give students a topic and ask them to think about how they would describe it to a friend, as Ms. Jay did in her lesson. Both activities illustrate the features of spoken English and facilitate comparisons with written standard English.

2. Have students look at examples of written standard English.

After addressing the conversational English that students use in their everyday lives, ask them to look at some examples of written standard English. I recommend choosing texts similar to the writing genre you're studying. If you're working with informational reports, as Ms. Jay's class was, ask the students to look at examples of reference materials. If your students are writing short stories, show them some stories and point out the examples of standard English in them. When talking with students about standard English use in fiction, I've used the opening line to the novel *Ralph S. Mouse*, by Beverly Cleary: "Night winds, moaning around corners and whistling through cracks, dashed snow against the windows of the Mountain View Inn" (Cleary, 1982, p.1). After reading this excerpt, I tell the students that the book's narrator presents the information in a formal way and ask the students what the narrator might say if casually telling this information to a friend. One student's phrasing of "Man, it was cold and windy at the Mountain View Inn" revealed his understanding of the differences between conversational and standard English.

3. Work with students to compare features and uses of spoken English and written English.

The next step is to work with students to compare the features and uses of conversational and standard English. Comparing both the features and the uses of each style of communication helps students understand *what* these kinds of language look like and *why* a writer would use each of them. I recommend working with the students to create T-charts for each topic. Guide students through a discussion of what conversational and standard English look like, and follow up by asking them why someone might use one or the other. Figures 5.2 (below) and 5.3 (page 54) depict examples of charts I've made while working with students on this concept and recording their ideas.

It's interesting to note the students' awareness of audience on the Uses chart, with friends and some family members identified as audiences for conversational English, and school and those in charge as the audiences for standard English.

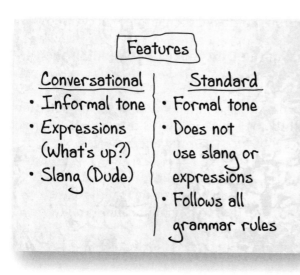

Figure 5.2 Features of Conversational and Standard English

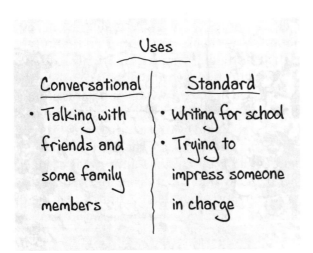

Figure 5.3 Uses of Conversational and Standard English

4. Help students apply their knowledge of these differences to their own writing.

Once you are comfortable with students' understandings of the features and uses of conversational and standard English, ask them to apply what they've learned to their writing. I recommend asking students to review the pieces they're currently writing to check for conversational and standard English. Ask students to label any examples of conversational English they notice. Though standard English is generally the style in which students are expected to write in school, there are times when writers will write in ways that reflect nonstandard spoken language, such as when writing dialogue. Therefore, conversational English doesn't always need to be eliminated from student writing. I suggest conferencing with students individually and discussing examples of conversational English in their writing. Doing so can help them determine whether that style of language is best suited for the audience and purpose of the particular piece of writing.

Final Thoughts on Recognizing the Differences Between Spoken and Written Standard English

The following information summarizes major points from this chapter, including what this grammatical concept is, why it's important for good writing, and how one might teach it for maximum effectiveness.

- ◆ Recognizing the differences between spoken and written standard English is included in Common Core Language Standard 3.3.
- ◆ Spoken English is often characterized by an informal, conversational style.
- ◆ Written standard English often represents "textbook" language in which grammatical rules and customs are followed.

♦ Knowing when to use standard English is important to effective writing; in many genres and circumstances, readers expect this form of English.

♦ The audience and purpose of a particular communication often determine the language the writer or speaker is expected to use.

♦ It is important that students know whether to use conversational English or standard English when they communicate with others.

♦ When teaching students about recognizing the differences between spoken and written standard English, try these four things:

- Activate students' prior knowledge about spoken English.
- Have students look at examples of written standard English.
- Work with students to compare the features and uses of the two.
- Help students apply their knowledge of these differences to their own writing.

Section **2**

Grammatical Concepts Aligned With Grade Four
Common Core Language Standards

6

Re-Envisioning Writing With Relative Pronouns and Relative Adverbs

What Are Relative Pronouns and Relative Adverbs?

Common Core Language Standard 4.1 addresses the study of relative pronouns and adverbs. As part of a more general statement that students should master conventions of speaking and writing, this standard calls for students to "use relative pronouns (*who, whose, whom, which, that*) and relative adverbs (*where, when, why*)" (Common Core Standards, 2010).

Relative pronouns and adverbs introduce relative clauses, which are important grammatical concepts to understand. Let's look at that sentence again: relative pronouns and adverbs introduce relative clauses, *which are important grammatical concepts to understand*. The italicized information in this sentence is a relative clause; it begins with the relative pronoun *which* and provides additional information to the sentence. Relative clauses are adjectival. This relative clause is actually describing the noun *relative clauses*; how's that for an application of grammar?!

It's important to emphasize that, whether a relative clause is introduced by a relative pronoun or a relative adverb, the clause still plays an adjectival role in the sentence. The fact that relative adverbs modify nouns, not verbs or adjectives, sometimes confuses students, so let's look at an example for clarification: I am excited for Monday, **when two ninjas will be visiting our school**.

In this sentence, *when* is a relative adverb and "when two ninjas will be visiting our school" is a relative clause. Even though *when* is an adverb, the information provided here modifies the noun *Monday*.

Figures 6.1 and 6.2 (page 60) summarize some key points regarding relative clauses, relative pronouns, and relative adverbs.

Figure 6.1 Relative Pronouns

Grammatical Concept	Relative Pronouns
What are they?	Pronouns that introduce relative clauses
What are some examples?	The relative pronouns are *who*, *whose*, *whom*, *which*, and *that*.
What do they look like in writing?	Bob, **who** is training for the World's Strongest Man competition, will help you move the couch. Note that *who* is a relative pronoun, and "who is training for the World's Strongest Man competition" is a relative clause.

Figure 6.2 Relative Adverbs

Grammatical Concept	Relative Adverbs
What are they?	Adverbs that introduce relative clauses
What are some examples?	The relative adverbs are *where*, *when*, and *why*.
What do they look like in writing?	If you walk past the pond and turn left, you will see the soccer field **where** our game will be played. Note that *where* is a relative adverb, and "where our game will be played" is a relative clause.

Why Relative Pronouns and Relative Adverbs Are Important to Good Writing

When talking with students about relative pronouns and adverbs, it's important to help them think of these grammatical concepts as tools that can make their writing better. Relative pronouns and relative adverbs are important because they can add important contextual information to a piece of writing. If a relative clause is removed from any sentence, the sentence will lack detail and information it previously had. Such information is often crucial to helping readers picture what is taking place in the sentence or understand a key element of the situation. The information included in relative clauses can give bland sentences a great deal more detail and meaning. A basic sentence such as "John flew in an airplane" takes on a much different tone when it is revised to read, "John, who has always been afraid of heights, flew in an airplane." Adding the relative clause "who has always been afraid of heights" alters readers' perceptions of the situation and provides information readers otherwise would not have. To further illustrate the importance of the concept, consider a sentence from Jerry

Spinelli's novel *Maniac Magee*. In the section from which this sentence is drawn, Maniac Magee, the new kid in town, is about to embarrass local baseball legend John McNab by hitting his supposedly unhittable pitch.

In the following passage, a relative adverb emphasizes how surprising Maniac's baseball success against McNab was (the relative clause is in bold type). "McNab fired. The kid swung. The batters in line automatically turned their eyes to the backstop, **where the ball should be**—but it wasn't there. It was in the air, riding on a beeline right out to McNab's head, the same line it came in on, only faster" (Spinelli, 1990, p. 24).

The relative adverb *where* plays a key role in this passage—it introduces a relative clause that signals a shift in the situation. Readers learn that the backstop was "where the ball should be" and then discover that the ball was actually flying in the other direction. Spinelli used the relative pronoun and clause to describe one of the heroic feats of Maniac Magee.

In the book *Because of Winn-Dixie*, Kate DiCamillo used relative pronouns to depict the narrator's attitude toward the other children around her. In this section, India (the book's protagonist and narrator) describes her negative attitude toward other children in her community.

> And there weren't that many kids at the Open Arms, just Dunlap and Stevie Dewberry. . . . And Amanda Wilkinson, **whose face was always pinched up like she was smelling something real bad**; and Sweetie Pie Thomas, **who was only five years old and still mostly a baby**. (DiCamillo, 2000, p. 38)

DiCamillo's use of relative clauses is especially effective—she used them to point out reasons India did not want to spend time with Amanda Wilkinson and Sweetie Pie Thomas. The relative pronouns in this passage focus readers' attention on characteristics that Amanda and Sweetie Pie possess.

Spinelli and DiCamillo show that relative pronouns and adverbs are writing tools that can add important details. Spinelli's relative clause directs attention to a backstop where a baseball surprisingly is not; the clauses DiCamillo used point out reasons the protagonist might not want to spend time with certain individuals.

Teachers can use these examples as models for students as they integrate relative pronouns and adverbs into their writing. Students shouldn't copy these relative clauses directly but rather use them as conceptual models when they create their own work. In other words, just as Spinelli and DiCamillo used relative clauses to add key pieces of information to their writing, so should students. Teachers will want to give them the necessary support and scaffolding to help them apply the concepts to their writing. In the next section of this chapter, we'll look inside a fourth-grade classroom in which a teacher named Ms. Walker employs an interactive and engaging lesson that helps her students understand the uses of relative pronouns and relative adverbs.

A Classroom Snapshot

On a rainy Monday morning, Ms. Walker's fourth graders trudge toward their desks. The only audible conversation concerns the previous day's professional football scores and a student's upcoming birthday party. A glance at the agenda written on the whiteboard reveals that grammar instruction will open the day's work. Student energy is low, but there are important grammatical concepts to discuss; Ms. Walker needs to make sure her students develop strong understandings of relative pronouns and relative adverbs.

Though this may not sound like a situation in which students will be especially attentive, Ms. Walker has it covered. The previous week, the students learned to identify relative pronouns and relative adverbs in connection with Common Core Language Standard 4.1. However, Ms. Walker knows that simply instructing students on these terms and asking them to commit them to memory will not be useful to the students in the long term. Before class began, she told me, "I want to make sure this information sticks with them." Commenting on grammar instruction in general as well as that particular day's lesson, she explained, "I want them to understand grammar because I think it's really important to do more than memorize it. I think today's lesson will help them get it."

The lesson to which Ms. Walker referred certainly helps students "get it"; it is engaging and interactive and helps students think metacognitively about why relative pronouns and adverbs can make a difference in writing. Ms. Walker steps to the front of the room and writes, "The bear walked toward Paul" on the board. She then thinks aloud about the sentence for the class: "When I look at this sentence," she begins, "I know something about what's going on, but there's so much I don't know."

A few students nod, so Ms. Walker asks one to share her thoughts.

The student says, "There's a lot more you could say, like how you tell us to put details in our writing. This sentence doesn't have a lot of details." Smiling, Ms. Walker affirms this statement and tells the students their job is to add those details. She reminds them of the work they did on relative pronouns and relative adverbs and instructs them on how to integrate that knowledge into the activity. "When you expand on this sentence, use either a relative pronoun or a relative adverb to introduce that information." After reviewing some sentences from the previous lesson and explaining that the relative pronouns and adverbs in those sentences introduce relative clauses, Ms. Walker prepares to turn the students loose. She explains that the 20-person class will break up into four groups, each of which will be responsible for providing additional information about the situation briefly outlined on the board. She explains further: "You can describe the bear or you can describe Paul, but your group needs to rewrite the sentence and add more information. Think of some different ways you can use relative pronouns or relative adverbs to give some more detail to what's happening in this sentence."

The students gather in their assigned groups, and Ms. Walker circulates around the room, answering questions about relative pronouns and relative adverbs and helping students hone their ideas. Sitting down with one group, she explains, "That's an interesting detail, but it doesn't begin with a relative pronoun or adverb. Let's look together at the relative pronouns and relative adverbs posted in the front of the room. Can you think of a way to change the rewrite so it begins with one of those words?"

After a bit of discussion, the group decides to change the sentence from "The hungry bear walked toward Paul" to "The bear, which hadn't eaten all day, walked toward Paul." When Ms. Walker asks the group members what they notice about the new sentence, a student offers, "There's a lot more detail. We know that the bear hasn't eaten all day, and that can be good to know." This student's comment reveals an understanding of how relative clauses can provide key details.

Shortly after this, the groups are ready to share their revised sentences, which are found in the table below.

Original Sentence: The bear walked toward Paul.	
Group 1	"The bear, which hadn't eaten all day, walked toward Paul."
Group 2	"The bear walked toward Paul, who was too close to the bear's cub."
Group 3	"The bear walked toward Paul, who had just started to eat lunch."
Group 4	"The bear, which liked the Cowboys, walked toward Paul, who was wearing a Redskins shirt."

After the groups share, Ms. Walker talks with the students about the ways the different relative clauses produced sentences with different meanings. She talks with the students about why writers use relative clauses, and a student volunteers his interpretation: "The relative clause you use makes a big difference. It can tell us why the bear walked toward Paul. The bear's reason could be a big deal—he could be mad or happy. The relative clause can show that."

Ms. Walker informs the students that they're building toward being able to pick out the relative clauses in writing and explain why they are important to the text. "It's like what we did today when we looked at these sentences," she states, "except you'll be doing it with a published author's writing and explaining why the author used the relative clause in the way he or she did." The students ask about different books they can use, with some inquiring about using books from the Harry Potter and Diary of a Wimpy Kid series. Ms. Walker explains that she will give additional instructions in the next class and says that she's glad the students are so excited. After the lesson, she tells me how pleased she is with the students' progress with relative pronouns and adverbs. "I can tell they're not only understanding the basic grammar of it but also thinking about why it's important to writing. They're doing great work. By the time we're done analyzing the literature, I think this will definitely stay with them."

Recommendations for Teaching Students to Use Relative Pronouns and Relative Adverbs

In this section, I describe two recommended instructional processes for teachers to use when teaching about relative pronouns and relative adverbs. Each was designed to help students understand why relative pronouns and relative adverbs are tools for effective writing. In each instance, I describe the process, address its importance, and provide step-by-step directions for implementing it. Because these processes are intended to be applications of the students' knowledge of relative pronouns and adverbs, it's important to use the information and examples in the beginning of this chapter to provide students with a basic overview of the concept before beginning the steps described.

Recommended Instructional Process 1: Expand

One aspect of Ms. Walker's lesson that most impressed me was the way it incorporated sentence expansion: she asked students to use relative pronouns and adverbs to build on a basic sentence. Grammar experts Don and Jenny Killgallon refer to the kind of information Ms. Walker's students added as "additions" and explain that "additions are the tools that skillful writers use to build their sentences" (Killgallon & Killgallon, p. 5). Expanding these basic sentences had two key benefits for Ms. Walker's students: (1) Students gained practice using relative pronouns and adverbs, and (2) students were able to see how the information they added shaped the meaning of the sentence. Each benefit is important for students as they begin to see grammatical concepts as tools that can be used to build effective sentences. As they practice implementing these concepts in their writing, they can consider how writing changes when new information is added.

Following is a step-by-step process, similar to the one Ms. Walker followed in her lesson, for helping your students use relative pronouns and relative adverbs to expand on existing sentences. These are the steps in this instructional process:

1. Present a basic sentence to the students.
2. Describe the relative pronouns and relative adverbs as "tools for change."
3. Turn the students loose.
4. Discuss the differences.

Depending on the individual needs of your students and the amount of time you feel they might need with each step, you can decide to space these activities out over multiple days or combine them into one day of instruction.

1. Present a basic sentence to the students.

As was the case in Ms. Walker's class, presenting a basic sentence provides the students with a starting point for using relative pronouns and adverbs. The basic nature of the sentence gives students an opportunity to expand it in a creative way while also providing the necessary structure for young writers who are still new to this grammatical concept. Basic sentences that provide opportunities for students to be a bit playful and creative (such as the one Ms. Walker presented about a bear) can be especially effective, as they can help provide a nonthreatening environment for students to practice with relative pronouns and adverbs.

2. Describe the relative pronouns and relative adverbs as "tools for change."

Although "tools for change" might sound as though it has more to do with a protest than it does with grammar instruction, it's certainly relevant to teaching this concept. After presenting a basic sentence to the students, the next step is to talk with them about how to use relative pronouns and adverbs to add key details and information. To do this, call attention to the basic nature of the original sentence and discuss how relative pronouns and adverbs can make it less basic through the information they can add. This is a good time to review the fundamentals of relative pronouns and adverbs and look at some examples of sentences that contain them, as this can ensure the students' clear understandings of what these concepts are.

3. Turn the students loose.

After providing students with these instructions and explanations, it's time to turn them loose and have them expand on the basic sentence by using relative pronouns and adverbs to add key details. This can be done in small groups, as Ms. Walker did with her class, or individually; either way, be sure to check in with students as they work and make sure they are using the grammatical concept correctly. These one-on-one or small-group interactions are sometimes the best times to clarify students' understanding and can be especially effective with students who aren't vocal or confident enough to ask questions in front of the whole class.

4. Discuss the differences.

One of my favorite parts of this activity is the opportunity to discuss the differences in students' sentences. Think back to the student in Ms. Walker's class who explained that relative clauses can influence the meaning of a sentence. This statement revealed a strong understanding of the different kinds of information that relative pronouns and adverbs can introduce. By asking students to discuss the differences in the ways they added relative pronouns and/or adverbs to a basic sentence, we can move them to similar levels of metacognition by showing them how much the information they added contributes to the meaning of the sentence. The details students add allows the sentence to take on a new form that focuses on a particular aspect or contains a specific piece of information. Discussing the differences between the sentences can ensure students' understanding of this important idea.

Recommended Instructional Process Two: Critique

Another effective practice for teaching this concept involves students' analyzing how and why authors use relative pronouns and adverbs in their writing. Ms. Walker referred to this activity at the end of her lesson as another way of helping students understand why relative pronouns and adverbs are important to good writing. By reviewing published authors' uses of this grammatical concept, students learn to think critically about why those authors chose to use it, why it's an important concept for good writing, and how students can apply it to their future writing.

Following is a step-by-step process for enabling students to engage in meaningful critiques of how published authors use relative pronouns and adverbs.

1. Send the students on a scavenger hunt.
2. Have students remove the relative clauses.
3. Tell students to swap the relative clauses.
4. Encourage students to consider the implications to their own writing.

This process can be done as a follow-up to the previous activity but does not need to be. It is intended to help students think critically about the power of this grammatical concept as well as the importance of thinking about the choices writers make and why they make them. As with the previous activity, you can decide whether to space the components of this lesson out over multiple days or combine them (depending on the needs and characteristics of your students).

1. Send the students on a scavenger hunt.

Before students critique relative pronouns and adverbs, they have to find them! I enjoy making this an interactive activity in which students look through children's books to find as many uses of relative pronouns and adverbs as they can. To facilitate this, I look through my classroom library beforehand and find as many books as possible that contain relative pronouns and adverbs. When it's time for the activity, I distribute the books to the students and tell them that we'll look through these books to locate as many sentences that use relative clauses as possible. To give my students a bit more support, I use post-it notes to mark specific chapters in which relative clauses appear. I like to have students work on this in pairs so they can communicate about whether a selection from the text actually is a relative clause; I believe they can learn a lot from communicating with each other about this, and I'm always circulating around the room in case my help is needed. As students do this, I also do my own scavenger hunt with a children's book so that I can talk with students about the relative pronouns and adverbs I find; I think students are more motivated to do this activity if they see me doing it as well.

2. Have students remove the relative clauses.

After students identify relative clauses in the scavenger hunt and share them with the class, we discuss what the selections from the texts would be like if the relative clauses they found were not there. To get this activity started, I show students two pieces of chart paper: one with the original sentence, including the relative clause, and the other with the relative clause removed. The image in Figure 6.3 (below) depicts a piece of chart paper I display in the classroom. A sentence from Matt Christopher's soccer novel *Top Wing* is printed on it: "The Cottoneer center had kicked the ball back to his halfback, **who aimed a kick to his right wing**" (Christopher, 1994, p. 23). This sentence contains the relative pronoun *who* and the relative clause "who aimed a kick to his right wing."

Figure 6.4 (page 68) also depicts a piece of chart paper, this one containing the same sentence but with the relative clause removed.

I put these sentences on chart paper to provide my students with a clear visual of how much the sentences vary without the relative clauses. After I post the visual in the classroom, I ask the students why they think Christopher may have chosen to use that relative clause. During one of these conversations, a student commented that "The relative clause is a big deal because it tells what happened next. Without it, we don't know if the halfback lost the ball or dribbled it or what, but with it we know that

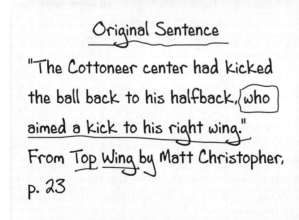

Figure 6.3 Original Sentence from *Top Wing*

> ### Sentence Without
> ### Relative Clause
>
> "The Cottoneer center had kicked the ball back to his halfback ..."

Figure 6.4 Sentence Without Relative Clause

he aimed it at the right wing." Another student added, "It wouldn't be as good a sentence without [the relative clause]. We wouldn't know those details." These students' comments demonstrate the ability to analyze the use of this relative clause; they show an understanding of its importance and impact on the piece.

After discussing this example with the students, I ask them to focus on the sentences they selected by considering what those sentences would be like without relative clauses. Students first discuss their observations in small groups before volunteers share with the whole class. In one of these discussions, a student noted:

> I used *The Little Prince*. The part that I found that had a relative clause goes like this: "I know full well that apart from the large planets, such as Earth, Jupiter, Mars and Venus, which have been given names, there are hundreds of others which are sometimes so small that it is difficult to see them through the telescope. When an astronaut discovers one of them, he does not give it a name but a number" (Saint-Exupery, 1943, p. 20).

This student observed that "'which have been given names' is the relative clause." When asked what the sentence would be like without that relative clause, the student reasoned, "Without that relative clause, it wouldn't point out that these planets have names and a bunch of others don't. The relative clause kind of compares them that way and helps make a point." Her comment revealed her awareness of not only what the relative clause does in this passage but also that the passage wouldn't have the same effect if the relative clause were removed.

3. Tell the students to swap the relative clauses.

After students remove the relative clauses from the passages they selected, I ask them to put them back in—but to swap them out for new relative clauses! In this activity, the students replace the relative clause in the passage with one that changes the meaning of the sentence. The goal of this activity is to further illustrate to students the importance of relative clauses by showing them that changing the relative clause in a piece can drastically impact its meaning. Replacing relative clauses can allow students to be creative and have some fun with this concept, while also emphasizing its importance to effective writing.

I like to begin the activity by returning to the sentence from Christopher's book *Top Wing* that I previously wrote on a piece of chart paper: "The Cottoneer center had kicked the ball back to his halfback, **who** aimed a kick to his right wing" (Christopher, 1994, p. 23). I review with the students why the relative clause is important to this sentence, describing the detail it adds to the sentence and pointing out that it tells readers what the halfback did next. I explain that we've already considered how the sentence would look without the relative clause, but we haven't yet talked about what it would be like with a *different* relative clause. I ask the students to work in groups and come up with replacements for the relative clause in this sentence.

After the students work together on this activity, I ask each group to share its replacement sentence. Here are the sentences created by a class of fourth graders with whom I recently worked.

- ◆ The Cottoneer center had kicked the ball back to his halfback, **who** wasn't paying attention.
- ◆ The Cottoneer center had kicked the ball back to his halfback, **who** was actually a secret agent.
- ◆ The Cottoneer center had kicked the ball back to his halfback, **who** was eating a hamburger.
- ◆ The Cottoneer center had kicked the ball back to his halfback, **who** missed it.

I record these sentences on a piece of chart paper and ask the students for their reactions. The groups are typically proud of their sentences and enjoy explaining how their sentences vary from the original text. A student from the group that created the sentence in which the halfback is a secret agent shared her analysis: "In the original sentence, the halfback did something you'd do in soccer. In ours, he did something totally different. Changing that [relative clause] made it all different." Her comments affirmed the importance of the information provided by relative clauses: these additional details can provide further clarification about a situation, but they can also take a piece in an entirely different direction, as was the case with the examples these students created.

4. Encourage students to consider implications to their own writing.

To wrap up the discussion of relative pronouns and adverbs, I ask students to reflect on how their understandings of these grammatical concepts can affect their own writing. To facilitate their reflections, I put the following discussion questions on the board:

- Why are relative clauses important?
- How can changing the relative clause in a piece of writing change the piece's meaning?
- How can you use relative clauses as tools in your future writing?

I use the first two questions as warm ups to build toward their responses to the third one. By the time they reach this point in the lesson, I know the students will be able to tell me why relative clauses are important and how changing them can alter the meaning of a piece. My goal is to close this series of activities with the students' telling me how they might use this concept in their future work. This shows me that they have developed a metacognitive awareness of the usefulness of this strategy. In addition, I want students to see grammatical concepts such as these not just as information they need to memorize but also as tools they can use as they write. Their responses to this question show me whether they are starting to look at grammar from this perspective.

In one such discussion, a student insightfully observed, "Relative clauses are great tools because they help the writer give details to the reader that [the writer feels] is important. The writer can just decide what details he or she wants to tell [reader] and then use a relative clause [to do so]." Another student in the same class looked forward to applying this concept to her own writing: "I've never used these [relative clauses] and I never knew what relative pronouns and relative adverbs were, but now I think using them can be great for my writing." These students' comments reveal a writerly perspective on relative pronouns and adverbs as well as the clauses they introduce; they indicate that the students are learning to see grammatical concepts as tools that can reshape writing.

Final Thoughts on Relative Pronouns and Relative Adverbs

The following information summarizes major points from this chapter, including what this grammatical concept is, why it's important for good writing, and how one might teach it for maximum effectiveness.

- Relative pronouns and relative adverbs are included in Common Core Language Standard 4.1.
- Relative pronouns and relative adverbs introduce relative clauses.
- The most commonly used relative pronouns are *who*, *whose*, *whom*, *which*, and *that*.

- ◆ The most commonly used relative adverbs are *where*, *when*, and *why*.
- ◆ Relative pronouns and relative adverbs can add important information and key details to writing.
- ◆ When teaching relative pronouns and relative adverbs, ask students to do these three things:
  - Use these concepts to expand on a basic sentence.
  - Consider how and why published authors use these concepts in their writing.
  - Reflect on how they might use relative pronouns and adverbs in their own written work.

7

The Progressive Verb Tenses and Why They Matter

What Are the Progressive Verb Tenses?

Common Core Language Standard 4.1 addresses the study of the progressive verb tenses, calling for students to "Form and use the progressive (e.g., *I was walking; I am walking; I will be walking*) verb tenses" (Common Core Standards, 2010) as part of a more general statement that students should show command of the conventions of speaking and writing.

Let's begin with an explanation of what the progressive verb tenses are and how they're similar to and different from some other verb tenses. When you think of verb tenses, you might think of past, present, and future. Though these are the most common tenses, other tenses add a little more detail to a writer's description of when an action takes place. For example, if you want to explain that an action is continuous or ongoing, you'd use one of the progressive verb tenses, which are ways of describing ongoing action. Though all the progressive forms describe continuous actions, there are three progressive verb tenses: the present progressive, past progressive, and future progressive. Let's examine each progressive tense individually so we can fully understand their similarities and differences.

The Present Progressive

The present progressive tense describes ongoing actions taking place in present time: "Dad **is walking** to the store." In this sentence, *is walking* is an example of the present progressive tense; it describes an ongoing action happening at the time of the statement. To form the present progressive tense, combine a present form of the verb *be* (*am, is,* or *are* depending on the style of the narration and the number of subjects) with the *-ing* form of a verb.

The Past Progressive

The past progressive tense describes actions that take place in the past over a continuous period, often at the same time something else occurred, as in the following example: "Dad **was walking** to the store when the aliens landed." In this sentence, *was walking* is an example of the past progressive tense; it shows that Dad walked for a continuous period at some point in the past. This sentence also shows us that the alien landing occurred during the time that Dad was walking. To form the past progressive tense, combine one the past forms of the verb *be* (*was* or *were* depending on whether the subject is singular or plural) with the *-ing* form of a verb.

The Future Progressive

The future progressive tense describes a continuous action that will take place in the future, such as "Dad **will be walking** to work every day until the car is fixed." In this example, *walking to work* is an ongoing action that Dad will be completing for an extended period. To create the future progressive tense, combine *will be* or *shall be* with the *-ing* form of a verb. In this tense, *be* does not change forms based on the narration or the number of subjects.

Figure 7.1 (below) outlines some key attributes of the past, present, and future progressive tenses.

Figure 7.1 The Progressive Verb Tenses

Tense	What It Does	What It Looks Like	How It's Formed
Present Progressive	Describes ongoing actions taking place at the present time	Dad *is walking* to the store.	Combine one of the present forms of be (*am*, *is*, or *are*) with the -ing form of a verb.
Past Progressive	Describes actions that took place in the past over a continuous period of time, often at the same time something else occurred	Dad *was walking* to the store when the aliens landed.	Combine one of the past forms of the verb be (*was* or *were*) with the -ing form of a verb.
Future Progressive	Describes continuous actions that will take place in the future	Dad *will be walking* to work every day until the car is fixed.	Combine *will be* or *shall be* with the -ing form of a verb.

Why the Progressive Verb Tenses Are Important for Good Writing

The progressive verb tenses are important tools for clear and effective writing because they allow authors to indicate the continuous nature of certain events. Whether these ongoing events happened in the past, are happening in the present, or will happen in the future, writers can add detail and meaning to their works by using this tense. This level of detail is difficult to achieve using only the basic past, present, and future tenses and can be important to readers' understanding of the text. To illustrate this point, let's look at Figure 7.2 (below), which shows how the verb *sprint* appears in the past, present, and future tenses compared to the forms it takes in the progressive tenses.

Published authors frequently take advantage of the additional levels of meaning and detail the progressive verb forms offer. In the book *The Batboy* (2010), author Mike Lupica used the past progressive to describe an ongoing action in the past and to explain that the action was taking place when another occurred: "As he and Finn were stacking the boxes of gum and sunflower seeds for the night, Brian said, 'I don't have a bat'" (p. 165). Lupica used the past progressive *were stacking* not only to indicate that this was a continuous action but also to show that this action provided the context for Brian's saying he didn't have a bat to use when the two boys were supposed to take batting practice on a major league baseball field.

Another example of an author utilizing a progressive verb is in *Diary of a Wimpy Kid: The Last Straw*. Greg, the book's narrator, discovers how much he likes bathrobes and then says, "Now I'm wondering what else I'm missing out on" (Kinney, 2009, p. 8). In this sentence, *I'm wondering* is written in the present progressive tense, indicating that Greg's wondering is an ongoing action that can continue indefinitely. The sentence suggests that Greg's surprise at how comfortable he finds bathrobes results in his continuously wondering what else he might enjoy.

Figure 7.2 Comparison of Verb Tenses

Tense	Form of *Sprint*
Present	I sprint.
Present Progressive	I am sprinting.
Past	I sprinted.
Past Progressive	I was sprinting.
Future	I will sprint.
Future Progressive	I will be sprinting.

These selections from *The Batboy* and *Diary of a Wimpy Kid: The Last Straw* show ways authors use progressive verb tenses when they want to indicate a continuous action. This concept is a tool that writers have in their grammar toolboxes to craft detailed pieces that convey specific meanings. Without progressive verb tenses, Lupica and Kinney would not have been able to describe the situations in their books as clearly as they did. When teachers present this concept to students, they want to help students understand how to apply it to their own writing.

In the next section, we'll again look inside Ms. Walker's class and see how she helps her students learn about and use progressive verb tenses.

A Classroom Snapshot

It's a beautiful Friday in Ms. Walker's class. The sun shines brightly through the classroom windows, and the students seem to be contemplating what they'll do this weekend. They've just finished a math test, and many start to fidget as Ms. Walker transitions to the next activity. However, this fidgeting will be short-lived, as they're about to take part in an engaging lesson about the progressive verb tenses.

Ms. Walker has organized her instruction of this concept into multiple days; earlier in the week, she showed her students examples of the progressive verb tenses and discussed their characteristics. Today's lesson was designed to build on the class's previous work—its objective is to increase the students' familiarity with this concept by giving them practice creating their own examples and reflecting on them. The ultimate goal is for students to understand what progressive verb tenses are and why writers use them.

Ms. Walker opens the lesson by standing in the front of the room and holding up two index cards. The students are immediately pulled in by this introduction: Previously wandering gazes seem to sharpen, and students who were slouching in their seats sit more attentively. She explains to the students, "On the index card in my left hand, I need a subject. It can be anything, any kind of noun you can think of."

"A platypus!" a student calls out. Ms. Walker smiles and some other students giggle.

"I'm writing *a platypus* on this card," responds Ms. Walker. "That will be my subject. Now I need a verb. Who has an idea for a verb?"

"Read," answers another student.

"OK," responds Ms. Walker, "on this card I'm writing *read*. We're going to create some descriptions of this platypus reading using each of the progressive verb tenses. Who can tell us something about those tenses?"

A number of students raise their hands; Ms. Walker calls on one near the back of the room, who says, "They talk about an ongoing action."

Ms. Walker nods, says that they'll start with the present progressive tense, and asks the students for an example of a sentence about a platypus reading using that tense. A few students raise their hands immediately, and several others follow. Ms. Walker calls on a girl who states, "The platypus is reading."

Ms. Walker compliments the student's response and writes on the board, "Present progressive: The platypus is reading." She follows up by asking the students for a version of this sentence in the past progressive tense. This time, many hands go up quickly. Ms. Walker pauses, perhaps slightly surprised by the enthusiastic response, and then calls on a student who has not yet spoken. He answers, "The platypus was reading."

"OK. That's a good start," replies Ms. Walker. She writes on the board, "Past progressive: The platypus was reading" and then asks the class, "Remember how writers sometimes use the past progressive to talk about two things that are happening at the same time?" Many students, including the one who just responded, reply in the affirmative. "Can someone give us an example of something that was happening at the same time that the platypus was reading?"

The same student volunteers, "Lightning struck the house."

Ms. Walker amends the sentence on the board to read, "Past progressive: The platypus was reading when lightning struck the house." "See the difference?" she asks her students. "This sentence says the platypus was reading and lightning struck during that time." She reminds the students of some other examples they looked at that week that have similar meanings.

"Now, how about the future progressive tense?" she asks. "Can anyone describe the platypus reading in the future progressive?"

This time, even more hands go up. Ms. Walker scours the room for students who have not yet contributed. She calls on a girl who answers, "The platypus will be reading."

Ms. Walker nods as she writes on the board, "Future progressive: The platypus will be reading." "This sentence," she explains, "shows us that the platypus will be reading for a continuous time in the future. We could add other details to it if we wanted to make it say, for example, 'The platypus will be reading all summer' or 'The platypus will be reading during the plane ride." Students chuckle at the description of the platypus's actions.

Ms. Walker explains that the students will now do a similar activity in groups. She tells the students that she's going to break them up into groups and that each group will pick a subject and a verb from two stacks of index cards she has—one stack is subjects, and the other is verbs. She tells them their job is to write a sentence in each of the three progressive tenses, using the subject and verb they select.

Ms. Walker organizes the 20 students into four groups of five and moves around the room, checking in with them as they get started. One group selects the subject *teachers* and the verb *sing*. When Ms. Walker asks members of this group about the sentences they've come up with, she challenges the students to revise their example of the past progressive tense to describe two actions taking place at the same time: "Remember the example we worked on together?" she asks. "We said something happened *while* the platypus was reading. Talk together and see if you can come up with a sentence that says something happened *while* the teachers were singing."

Ms. Walker walks away from that group and sits down next to another group, listening to students' ideas and offering feedback. After some time has passed, all the groups are ready to share their sentences. The "teachers singing" group goes first; here are the sentences they share with the class.

Present Progressive:	The teachers are singing today.
Past Progressive:	The teachers were singing when the power went out.
Future Progressive:	The teachers will be singing all day tomorrow.

Ms. Walker nods, pleased with the students' work. She praises the additional information this group added to the past progressive sentence: "Saying that the teachers were singing when the power went out adds some important detail because it tells us something that happened when they were singing." The students smile, proud of their work.

After the other groups share, Ms. Walker writes the following question on the board: "Why do writers use progressive verb tenses?" She looks at the class and then reads the question aloud. Student hands rise all over the room, and Ms. Walker calls on a girl in the front of the room.

"They show that something's ongoing," the student explains.

"OK," says Ms. Walker, "but why is showing that something is ongoing important?"

The same student replies, "I might want to say that I'm going to keep doing something, like I'm going to be talking on the phone all night, so my little brother should stay out of my room."

When I spoke with Ms. Walker later that week, she explained that the students seemed to have grasped progressive verb tenses: "They can create them in their own writing," she explained, "and they're able to explain what the progressive verb tenses mean. They know that these tenses describe ongoing actions, and they use them correctly."

Recommendations for Teaching Students About the Progressive Verb Tenses

In this section, I describe a step-by-step instructional process to use when teaching students about the progressive verb tenses:

1. Show students literary examples of the progressive verb tenses.
2. Discuss why the writers of those pieces chose to use the progressive verb tenses.

3. Have students create their own examples.
4. Ask students to use progressive verb tenses in their writing.

These steps can be implemented over multiple days of instruction. Since these instructional steps are intended to help students reflect on the progressive verb tenses and apply their knowledge of this concept, it's important to provide students with a basic overview of the concept using the information and examples in the beginning of this chapter before beginning the steps described.

1. Show students literary examples of the progressive verb tenses.

I recommend showing students examples from children's literature of each progressive verb tense; doing so shows that professional authors use these verb tenses and helps students examine this grammatical concept in the context of good writing, not just as something they need to memorize. In addition, showing students these examples sets the stage for the next step, in which students discuss how the progressive tenses enhance these works. Figure 7.3 (below) shows some examples from literature of each of the progressive tenses that I've shown students.

2. Discuss why these authors chose to use progressive verb tenses.

After showing students examples of each progressive tense, the next step is to discuss the benefits of using these tenses. I like to approach this by explaining to students that there are no accidents in good writing; everything writers do, they do with specific reasons in mind. I then remind students that the key element of the progressive tenses is that they describe

Figure 7.3 Examples of Progressive Tenses in Literature

Tense	Example	Text
Present Progressive	"*We're heading* down to see where the earth is forming a new seafloor" (Stamper, 2003, p. 56).	*Voyage to the Volcano*, by Judith Stamper
Past Progressive	"D.J. skipped up the thirty flights of stairs to Mrs. Jewl's room. He *was grinning* from ear to ear, from nose to chin, from here to there, and back again" (Sachar, 1985, p. 71).	*Sideways Stories from Wayside School*, by Louis Sachar
Future Progressive	"I *shall be writing* tonight for the last time" (White, 1952, p. 138).	*Charlotte's Web*, by E. B. White

continuous, or ongoing, action. We'll look at each example in Figure 7.3 and describe why it's important to know that each action is continuous. For example, when discussing the present progressive example from *Voyage to the Volcano*, I'll point out that the continuous action is *heading* and ask the students why the author described this action as ongoing. During one such conversation with a group of fourth graders, one student explained, "[*Heading*] was ongoing because it's something that was happening when [the character] was talking. It was going on when [the character] said it." When talking about the past progressive example from *Sideways Stories from Wayside School*, another student explained that *grinning* is the continuous action in the sentence because "The author wanted to show that D.J. was grinning the whole time he skipped up the stairs. He did it the whole time, so that makes it ongoing."

3. Have students create their own examples.

After students analyze why authors in selected published works use the progressive tenses, it's time to give them a chance to create their own. I recommend asking students to create sentences in the past, present, and future progressive tenses. Students can do this activity individually or in groups, as Ms. Walker's class did. I suggest asking students to use the same subject and verb for each sentence (as Ms. Walker did in her lesson); this helps students see that the sentences are similar in some ways and different in others. While the students create these sentences, check in with them to gauge their progress. Once you're pleased with their work, you can ask them to share their sentences. As the students share, I recommend asking them to continue to think about how these tenses are different and why they would use each one; this further strengthens the connection between this concept and good writing.

4. Ask students to use progressive verb tenses in their writing.

The final step is to ask students to use progressive verb tenses in their own writing. This step is important because it requires that students put into practice the knowledge they've gained about these tenses. I recommend asking students to write short fictional scenarios that use all three progressive verb tenses. This gives students additional practice using the tenses and requires them to use them in the context of an actual piece of writing. Using the tenses in context helps the students understand the benefits and enhances their awareness of why writers use them. If students practice in a supported setting, they can more easily apply their knowledge of these tenses to future pieces of writing.

Final Thoughts on the Progressive Verb Tenses

The following information summarizes major points from this chapter, including what this grammatical concept is, why it's important for good writing, and how one might teach it for maximum effectiveness.

- ◆ The progressive verb tenses are included in Common Core Language Standard 4.1.
- ◆ There are three progressive verb tenses: the past progressive, present progressive, and future progressive.
- ◆ The progressive verb tenses describe continuous, or ongoing, actions.
- ◆ The progressive verb tenses are important tools for effective writing because they allow authors to indicate the continuous nature of certain events.
- ◆ When teaching students about the progressive verb tenses, do these four things:
  - Show students literary examples of the progressive verb tenses.
  - Discuss why the writers of those pieces chose to use the progressive verb tenses.
  - Have students create their own examples.
  - Ask students to use progressive verb tenses in their writing.

8

Why Writers Use
Modal Auxiliaries

What Are Modal Auxiliaries?

Common Core Language Standard 4.1 addresses the study of modal auxiliaries, calling for students to "Use the modal auxiliaries (e.g., *can*, *may*,
must) to convey various conditions" (Common Core Standards, 2010). In
this chapter, we will examine what modal auxiliaries are and why they're
important tools for effective writing.

The modal auxiliaries are *will*, *would*, *shall*, *should*, *can*, *could*, *may*, *might*,
must, and *ought to*. These words are verbs used (together with other verbs)
to "convey conditions of probability, possibility, obligation, or necessity"
(Kolln & Funk, 2009, p. 75). For example, combining *cook* with various
modal auxiliaries yields different situations depending on which modal
auxiliary is used. "I will cook" suggests a different circumstance than
"I should cook." In the first sentence, the speaker is expressing definite
plans to cook; in the second sentence, that person may feel a responsibility
to cook but ultimately decide not to. Another example is "I must cook,"
which suggests that the speaker is required to cook and does not have a
choice. Figure 8.1 (page 84) summarizes some major points about modal
auxiliaries.

Why Modal Auxiliaries Are Important to Good Writing

Modal auxiliaries are important tools for effective writing; without them,
writers would have difficulty accurately describing particular situations.
For example, modal auxiliaries let readers know how likely it is that something will occur ("I **might** go" vs. "I **will** go") and whether the speaker is
being forced to do something ("I **can** do it" vs. "I **must** do it"). Because of

Figure 8.1 Modal Auxiliaries

Grammatical Concept	Modal Auxiliaries
What are they?	Verbs used (together with other verbs) to convey certain conditions
What are some examples?	The modal auxiliaries are *will, would, shall, should, can, could, may, might, must,* and *ought to*.
What do they look like in examples?	I *will* go the party after I eat lunch. I *should* to the party, but I don't want to. I *can* go to the party because I've finished my chores. I *must* go to the party because my parents are making me.

the impact modal auxiliaries can have on a meaning of a piece, it's important that writers not only use them but also use them correctly. Replacing one modal auxiliary with another and comparing the resulting meanings illustrates the power of modal auxiliaries. The sentence "I should learn Spanish" creates a much different situation than "I must learn Spanish" does. In the sentence with *must*, the speaker feels required to learn Spanish; the sentence containing *should* suggests learning Spanish would be a good idea.

To further illustrate the importance of modal auxiliaries, let's look at how published writers use them and how the meanings of their works would change with different modal auxiliaries. In Thomas Rockwell's novel *How to Eat Fried Worms*, a character named Billy says that if he were to ride his motorized minibike into church, "My parents would kill me" (Rockwell, 1988, p. 28). This sentence contains the modal auxiliary *would*, which illustrates that Billy believes his parents would definitely kill him if he were to hypothetically ride his minibike into church. If the sentence read, "My parents *might* kill me," Billy would be expressing uncertainty about what would happen. This phrasing isn't as strong as the original usage; it leaves room for doubt about the outcome.

In his novel *Catch That Pass*, Matt Christopher used the modal auxiliary *ought to* to explain that something is likely to happen. After main character Jim Nardi scores an important touchdown, the narrator states, "Boy, scoring that touchdown at the crucial moment made him feel great. That ought to shut up Dil and Hook for a while" (Christopher, 1989, p. 47). Changing the modal auxiliary in this sentence would also change how likely it would be that scoring a touchdown would quiet Dil and Hook, two of Jim's teammates who criticized his play. For example, replacing *ought to* with *will* creates a different sentence: in the new sentence, it's a certainly that a touchdown will quiet Dil and Hook. Alternatively, the modal auxiliary could be changed to something less certain than *ought to*, such as *could*. The sentence "That *could* shut up Dil and Hook" suggests that it's possible, but not necessary likely, that scoring the touchdown will have this effect.

Without modal auxiliaries, Rockwell and Christopher would not have been able to express the probability of certain events' taking place. Rockwell's use of the modal auxiliary *would* shows how upset Billy's parents would be if Billy rode his minibike into church, and Christopher's use of *ought to* indicates that Jim's touchdown probably quiets his detractors. In these examples, modal auxiliaries are important tools that allow writers to express what they want to say. In both cases, changing the modal auxiliaries altered the meanings of the sentences. When teachers discuss modal auxiliaries with students, they will want to help them understand what modal auxiliaries are, why they're important, and how changing them can have an impact on a piece's meaning. Let's look at how Ms. Walker helps her fourth-grade students understand the importance of modal auxiliaries.

A Classroom Snapshot

Ms. Walker's students seem amused. She's just written "I might play basketball after school today" on the whiteboard, with no further explanation. Smiling, one young man says, "Really Ms. Walker? I'll pick you for my team. How's your shooting?"

Ms. Walker smiles back, then says, "My son told me this over breakfast this morning. It's related to what we're going to be talking about today." The students cast confused looks at one another; one asks another if they're going to be playing basketball with Ms. Walker's son that day.

"No, we're not playing basketball today," laughs Ms. Walker. "I want to show you something about this sentence." She directs the students to the word *might* and explains that it is a key word in this sentence. "If I change this word," she explains, "I can change a lot about the sentence."

She rewrites the sentence on the board (below the previous one) so it reads, "I will play basketball after school today" and asks the students how the new sentence is different from the previous one.

"This [new sentence] says *will*," responds a student, "so it's going to happen."

Ms. Walker nods and responds, "The word *will* changes the meaning. *Might* means something can happen. *Will* means it definitely is going to happen. These words, *might* and *will*, are part of a group of words called the modal auxiliaries."

Ms. Walker distributes a handout to the students. It says Modal Auxiliaries on the top and lists each of the modal auxiliaries underneath. As she does this, she explains that she is giving them a list of all the modal auxiliaries. "These are all words you can use to show something about a situation," she explains. "You might use one of these words to show how likely it is that something will happen, as in our example about playing basketball after school." She takes a few minutes and discusses all the modal auxiliaries (*will, would, shall, should, can, could, may, might, must,* and *ought to*) with the students, noting differences in their meanings.

Then Ms. Walker tells the students they're going to look at how some writers use modal auxiliaries in the books they've written. She distributes a handout headed Examples from Literature of Modal Auxiliaries. Underneath the heading are the following two excerpts from children's novels:

1. "Mom looked me straight in the eye. 'Because your father will never grow up,' she said." (from *Dear Mr. Henshaw*, by Beverly Cleary)
2. "He could dance to pay for what I ate." (from *The Miraculous Journey of Edward Tulane*, by Kate DiCamillo)

Ms. Walker reads the sentences aloud as the students follow along and then asks if anyone can locate the modal auxiliary in the first sentence. She encourages the students to look at the handout she gave them with the modal auxiliaries on it before responding.

The students look over this sheet and then several raise their hands. Ms. Walker calls on a student who says, "The modal auxiliary is *will*."

"That's right," responds Ms. Walker. "Let's think about what this sentence would be like with a different modal auxiliary. Can someone tell us another one?"

A student raises his hand and asks, "How about *might*?"

"OK. Let's try it with *might*," replies Ms. Walker. She writes on the board, "Mom looked me straight in the eye. 'Because your father might never grow up,' she said." Ms. Walker underlines *might* to make it stand out to the students. "How is saying someone *might* never grow up different from saying they *will* never grow up?"

One student volunteers a response: "*Might never* means it's still possible. *Will never* means it can't happen. There's no chance."

Ms. Walker nods and elaborates on the student's statement, further discussing the meanings of those modal auxiliaries. She then tells the students to turn their attention to the next sentence on the handout ("He could dance to pay for what I ate."). She asks them to rewrite this sentence from *The Miraculous Journey of Edward Tulane* with a different modal auxiliary.

The students work on this, and Ms. Walker moves around the room, looking to see if anyone needs help. Once all students appear to have finished, Ms. Walker asks if anyone would like to share a response with the class.

Many hands shoot into the air; Ms. Walker calls on a student toward the back of the room, who says, "I wrote, 'He must dance to pay for what I ate.'"

"You changed the modal auxiliary to *must*," replies Ms. Walker. "How do you think this changes the meaning?"

"Now he *has* to dance," the student answers. "Before, it was something that just *could* happen."

Recommendations for Teaching Students About the Modal Auxiliaries

In this section, I describe a step-by-step instructional process to use when teaching students about modal auxiliaries:

1. Show students examples of modal auxiliaries from literature.
2. Have students change the modal auxiliaries in these works and discuss the new meanings.
3. Ask students to create their own examples of modal auxiliaries.
4. Have students change these examples and analyze the changes.

These steps were designed to help students understand the power that modal auxiliaries can have on a piece of writing. By changing modal auxiliaries and discussing the impact of those changes, students can learn why this grammatical concept is an important tool for good writing. Before beginning these steps, make sure to provide students with an overview of modal auxiliaries using the information at the beginning of this chapter.

1. Show students examples of modal auxiliaries from literature.

After you introduce the basic elements of modal auxiliaries, I recommend showing students examples of how published writers use this concept. Doing this lets students see what modal auxiliaries look like in practice and helps illustrate the importance of this grammatical concept to good writing. I recommend providing students with a handout, as Ms. Walker did, of examples from published texts. Notice how Ms. Walker's examples used different modal auxiliaries; this is an effective practice because it shows students that writers use a variety of modal auxiliaries and provides opportunities to compare the sentences. Any of the examples of modal auxiliaries from this chapter can be good ones to show fourth graders.

2. Have students change the modal auxiliaries and discuss the new meanings.

I recommend asking students to change published sentences by replacing the modal auxiliaries. Replacing the modal auxiliaries in these sentences allows students to compare the new sentences with the existing ones and helps them understand how much modal auxiliaries can impact the meaning of a piece. For example, Ms. Walker and her students changed the statement "Because your father **will** never grow up" from Beverly Cleary's novel *Dear Mr. Henshaw* to "Because your father **might** never grow up" and discussed that the modal auxiliary *might* creates a different situation than *will* does. To help students do this activity, I recommend doing an example with them and discussing it as a class. If the students seem to be comfortable with the concept, have them work in small groups or individually to change the modal auxiliaries in other sentences.

3. Ask students to create their own examples of modal auxiliaries.

After students have changed the modal auxiliaries in published works, ask them to create their own sentences that include modal auxiliaries. This gives students practice using modal auxiliaries in their own writing, which is important because they should ultimately be able to apply this concept to their own work. Before students create these sentences, I recommend reminding them of the variety of modal auxiliaries and the wide range of meanings they represent. You can do this by reviewing the published works they changed and the new meanings that resulted. This can help emphasize that writers use different modal auxiliaries depending on the message they want to communicate.

4. Have students change these examples and analyze the changes.

Finally, ask students to change the examples they created and analyze the new meanings those changes created. This is similar to what the students did with the published works, except this time they will use their own writing. Because the students will change their own work, they will see how much modal auxiliaries alter the meaning of writing. I recommend providing students with a form that asks them to write the original sentence and the changed sentence, each with the modal auxiliary underlined, and then analyze the differences in the meanings of the two sentences. Figure 8.2 (page 89) is an example of one student's work on this kind of activity. Note that the student used different modal auxiliaries to vary the meanings of the sentences he wrote. His first sentence states that Congress declared the Continental Army **would** be made up of volunteer soldiers; his revised version of that sentence states that Congress declared the Continental Army **ought to** be made up of volunteer soldiers. His follow-up response shows his understanding of the difference in the meanings of these two passages. He explains that changing *would* to *ought to* changes the statement from something that **will** happen to something that someone believes **should** happen.

Access the supplemental downloads (see page iv) for a blank, reproducible version of the form used for the student work in Figure 8.2.

Final Thoughts on Modal Auxiliaries

The following information summarizes major points from this chapter, including what this grammatical concept is, why it's important for good writing, and how one might teach it for maximum effectiveness.

- ◆ Modal auxiliaries are included in Common Core Language Standard 4.1.
- ◆ The modal auxiliaries are *will, would, shall, should, can, could, may, might, must,* and *ought to.*

Figure 8.2 Student Modal Auxiliary Activity

Sentence containing a modal auxiliary

The Congress voted to call the troops the Continetal Army and declared it <u>would</u> be made up of volunteer soldiers from each of the thirteen colonies.

Sentence with the modal auxiliary replaced

The Congress voted to call the troops the Continental Army and declared it <u>ought to</u> be made up of volunteer soldiers from each of the thirteen colonies.

How did changing the modal auxiliary change the meaning of the sentence?

By changing would into ought to, ought to means an opinion and would means shall, or will be happening.

♦ The modal auxiliaries are verbs used (together with other verbs) to "convey conditions of probability, possibility, obligation, or necessity" (Kolln & Funk, 2009, p. 75).

♦ Changing the modal auxiliary in a sentence can alter its meaning. For example, something that **can** happen can become something that **must** happen.

♦ When teaching modal auxiliaries, remember to do the following:
  • Show students examples of modal auxiliaries from literature.
  • Have students change the modal auxiliaries in these works and discuss the new meanings.
  • Ask students to create their own examples.
  • Have students change these examples and analyze the changes.

9

Remaking Writing With Prepositional Phrases

What Are Prepositional Phrases?

Common Core Language Standard 4.1 calls for students to "Form and use prepositional phrases" (Common Core, 2010). A prepositional phrase is a group of words that begins with a preposition and ends with a noun or pronoun, which is called the object of the preposition. Prepositions are used to show relationships between words in a sentence, such as where something is located or when something happened. For example, in the sentence "I ran across the street," "across the street" is a prepositional phrase; *across* is the preposition and *street* is the object of the preposition. In this sentence, the prepositional phrase tells readers where the person ran. Prepositional phrases can also tell when something happened, as in the following example: "After the game, we ate ice cream." In this example, "after the game" is the prepositional phrase; *after* is the preposition and *game* is the object of the preposition.

To create and use prepositional phrases, students need to know what prepositions are. Figure 9.1 (below) is a list of 20 frequently used prepositions to get students started thinking about this concept.

Figure 9.1 20 Frequently Used Prepositions

above	behind	down	in	over
across	beside	during	near	to
after	between	for	past	under
before	by	from	on	with

Figure 9.2 Prepositional Phrases

Grammatical Concept	Prepositional Phrases
What is a prepositional phrase?	A *prepositional phrase* is a group of words that begins with a preposition and ends with a noun or pronoun, which is called the object of the preposition.
What are some examples?	Some examples of prepositional phrases are • *behind the house* • *near the school* • *after the show*
What do they look like in examples?	We are having a picnic **behind the house.** I will meet you **near the school**. **After the show**, he took a nap.

Armed with knowledge of prepositions, students can practice forming prepositional phrases and ultimately applying them to their writing. Figure 9.2 (above) summarizes some key points regarding prepositional phrases:

Why Prepositional Phrases Are Important to Good Writing

Writers use prepositional phrases to add detail to their work, expanding on basic sentences so they provide readers with more information. If prepositional phrases are removed from a sentence, it will probably still make sense, but it won't have the same level of detail. Test this with a sentence from Figure 9.2: "We are having a picnic **behind the house**." If the prepositional phrase **behind the house** is removed, the sentence just says, "We're having a picnic." This new sentence still makes sense, but it no longer tells readers where the picnic is taking place. Depending on the situation, the location of this picnic could be very important. Perhaps no one is allowed in front of the house, so the picnickers decided to have a picnic behind the house instead. Writers can use prepositional phrases to express such information clearly.

Some published writers use prepositional phrases to add details to their work. In *Encyclopedia Brown Sets the Pace*, Donald J. Sobol used a prepositional phrase when describing Encyclopedia Brown and his partner, Sally Kimball, investigating a possible crime at a dog show: "Encyclopedia and Sally wandered among the dogs" (Sobol, 1982, p. 29). Without the prepositional phrase, this sentence would read "Encyclopedia and Sally wandered." Although this shorter sentence still makes sense, it doesn't explain that these two detectives were walking among the dogs. Without this prepositional phrase, the sentence would be vague; readers wouldn't know where the characters wandered: in the parking lot? near the concession stand? somewhere else? The prepositional phrase **among the dogs** provides an important detail about where this action took place.

Prepositional phrases are so important to good writing that sometimes writers use two of them in one sentence, as in this example from Jack Gantos's book *Joey Pigza Loses Control*: "In the morning Dad came into my room" (Gantos, 2000, p. 34). The first prepositional phrase, **in the morning**, tells readers when this event took place, and **into my room** tells where it happened. Without these prepositional phrases, the entire sentence would be "Dad came," a basic sentence lacking in detail. Gantos used these two prepositional phrases to provide important details and give readers a much clearer picture of what's going on.

As Sobol's and Gantos's examples illustrate, prepositional phrases are important tools for adding details to writing. Prepositional phrases aren't necessary for sentences to exist—all the examples we've discussed would be functional sentences with or without prepositional phrases. However, those sentences would be very vague and lacking in detail if the authors had not chosen to include at least one prepositional phrase to provide important information. In her fourth-grade classroom, Ms. Walker helps her students understand the importance of prepositional phrases.

A Classroom Snapshot

As Ms. Walker's students enter the classroom, many chuckle as they notice what's written on the whiteboard. After waiting a few minutes for the students to put away their things and find their seats, Ms. Walker directs her students to the following excerpt from Carl Hiaasen's novel *Chomp* written on the board: "Her dad was furiously chasing her around the Walmart parking lot . . ." (Hiaasen, 2012, p. 122).

"It's kind of a funny place to chase someone," Ms. Walker says, smiling, as more of the students laugh, "but this sentence has a lot to do with what we're studying: prepositional phrases."

In the past two classes, Ms. Walker and her students have discussed prepositional phrases by talking about high-frequency prepositions and the structure of a prepositional phrase. In today's class, they're going to talk about why prepositional phrases are especially useful for making writing effective.

"Can someone help us find a prepositional phrase here?" asks Ms. Walker, pointing to the text written on the board. Approximately half of the 20 students raise a hand; Ms. Walker calls on a student who correctly identifies **around the Walmart parking lot** as a prepositional phrase. Ms. Walker explains why she wrote that excerpt on the board. "I wanted you to see an example of a prepositional phrase," she says, "but I also want you to notice that this is from a published book." She continues to explain that professional writers frequently use prepositional phrases to add detail to the things they write, such as where or when something happened.

Next, Ms. Walker asks the students how this excerpt from *Chomp* would read without the prepositional phrase. A student raises his hand and states, "Her dad was furiously chasing her." Ms. Walker praises his response and asks a follow-up question: "How do you think that's different from what's written on the board?"

The student responds, "It doesn't tell you where he's chasing her."

Ms. Walker nods as she points to **around the Walmart parking lot** from the original text. She explains that the prepositional phrase, although only a few words long, is important because it says where the event is happening.

"Now, what do you think would happen if someone changed the prepositional phrase?" Ms. Walker asks. The students are silent at first, so she asks a follow-up question: "Would the sentence be the same?"

"No," a student responds, "it would be different."

Ms. Walker asks how it would be different, to which the student replies, "Like, it could say he chased her somewhere else instead of the Walmart parking lot."

Ms. Walker nods vigorously and builds off this student's response, explaining to the class that changing the prepositional phrase could state that the action happened somewhere else or even at a different time. "The sentence might say 'Her dad was furiously chasing her after dinner.' That would tell us when this happened," she states. Ms. Walker organizes the students into groups of five and says that each group will use a different prepositional phrase to write a new version of the excerpt from *Chomp*.

The students begin working, and Ms. Walker circulates around the room, listening to discussions and commenting when necessary. She walks past me and remarks at how well the students are doing. "They're all creating good prepositional phrases," she notes, "and there's a really nice variety too."

Once she has checked with each group, Ms. Walker announces that it's time to share the results of the activity. She calls on individual groups to share their new passages, each of which is listed in the following table.

Original Passage: "Her dad was furiously chasing her around the Walmart parking lot. . . ."	
Group 1	"Her dad was furiously chasing her past the Kmart."
Group 2	"Her dad was furiously chasing her before sunrise."
Group 3	"Her dad was furiously chasing her during lunchtime."
Group 4	"Her dad was furiously chasing her into the school."

Ms. Walker notes that two groups used prepositional phrases to say *where* this event took place, and two others used them to express *when*, explaining that this emphasizes the wide range of details prepositional phrases can add. She concludes by telling the students that, in future classes, they'll be talking more about adding prepositional phrases to their writing and that doing so can add important information to the texts they create.

Recommendations for Teaching Students About Prepositional Phrases

In this section, I describe a step-by-step instructional process to use when teaching students about prepositional phrases:

1. Show students how published authors use prepositional phrases.
2. Help students remove the prepositional phrases in published pieces and substitute new ones.
3. Have students add prepositional phrases to examples of "bland" writing.
4. Ask students to look for ways to apply prepositional phrases to their own work.

This instructional process was designed to help students understand that prepositional phrases are important tools writers use to add detail to their works. Each step is intended to illustrate that altering the prepositional phrases in a piece can change its meaning and level of detail. Because these steps were designed to help students apply their understanding of prepositional phrases, use the information at the beginning of this chapter to ensure that students understand the fundamentals of prepositions and prepositional phrases before beginning this instructional process.

1. Show students how published authors use prepositional phrases.

I recommend beginning by showing students examples of how published writers use prepositional phrases in their work. Providing examples of works that are enhanced by prepositional phrases helps students understand the important tool that prepositional phrases can be. Talk with students about the kinds of details the prepositional phrases add. For example, do they tell where an event took place? Do they explain when it happened? Asking questions such as this helps students consider the kinds of information prepositional phrases can add to a sentence. Many kinds of texts, ranging from picture books to novels, contain prepositional phrases. The examples of published texts that contain prepositional phrases featured in this chapter can work well with many fourth-grade classes, but I also encourage you to find some examples that might be especially interesting to your students.

2. Help students remove the prepositional phrases in published pieces and substitute new ones.

I recommend working with the students to help them remove the prepositional phrase (or phrases) in the published examples and substitute new ones. Removing them helps the students see how much detail prepositional phrases provide, and substituting new ones shows how much changing this information can alter a sentence's meaning. First, ask the students what the published sentence you've shown them would be like without its prepositional phrase. Then write that sentence next to the original one so the students can clearly see the difference. When recently working with a group of fourth graders on prepositional phrases, I placed a book on the document projector so the students could clearly see its title: *It Happened on a Train*. This book, one of the Brixton Brothers mysteries by Mac Barnett, has a prepositional phrase in its title. I wrote the title on the board and then asked the students what it would be like without that prepositional phrase. We discussed that the adjusted title, *It Happened*, would not provide nearly as much detail as the existing title. Though *It Happened on a Train* suggests to readers that some kind of important event took place on a train, *It Happened* doesn't really provide any kind of interesting or useful information.

After you work with the students to remove the prepositional phrase from the text you've selected, ask them to replace the old prepositional phrase with a new one. This can be done individually or in small groups. Ms. Walker's students did this in small groups in her lesson; you'll want to make the decision you feel best fits the personality of your class. When I did this activity with *It Happened on a Train*, students worked individually and created a range of examples, including "It Happened With a Zombie" and "It Happened During My Swim Meet." After your students create their examples, make sure you discuss the new meanings with them, including what kinds of details the prepositional phrases add and whether those prepositional phrases tell where or when an event took place.

3. Have students add prepositional phrases to examples of "bland" writing.

One effective way to help students understand the usefulness of prepositional phrases is to present them with an example of "bland" writing and have them add details to it, using prepositional phrases to add some of those details. When I do this with students, I create a short, basic text with very little description and ask students to rewrite it with more detail, using at least three prepositional phrases in their rewrites and underlining the prepositional phrases. After the students expand on the original text, I ask them to reflect on the differences between the pieces.

Figure 9.3 (page 97) shows Henry's work on this activity; he turned the original text into an entertaining and detailed story that includes a variety of prepositional phrases, such as "at a monster," "on his lawn," and "to the crimestoppers station."

The supplemental downloads that accompany this book (see page iv) include a template for this activity for your own use.

After students have completed this activity, ask them to share their passages. If you have access to a document projector, I recommend having students place their work on it so the others can follow along and take

Excerpt from "Billy's Adventure"

Billy stared. He started to run. He couldn't believe it. Billy stopped and looked again. Then he continued to run.

Your Rewrite, With At Least Three Prepositional Phrases

Billy stared at a huge monster on his lawn. He started to run to the crime stoppers station. He couldn't beleave it because the monster was one of them! Billy stopped and looked again at the monsters in the station. Then he continued to run away from the monsters. He saw they had candy in their hands. Then he realized it was October, the month of Halloween.

Your Reflection on the Differences

- It added more action.
- It added more interest.

note of the prepositional phrases included in their peers' texts. This can further help students understand the different kinds of details prepositional phrases can add, offering another illustration of how using different prepositional phrases can totally reshape the meaning of a piece. Once the students have discussed the examples they've created and the prepositional phrases in them, I recommend asking the students to consider, in writing, how prepositional phrases can help writers improve their work. Figure 9.4 (page 98) shows Henry's response to the question "In your own words, how can prepositional phrases help writers improve their works?" He notes that prepositional phrases can add more details to an existing passage and add more "interest/action."

4. Ask students to look for ways to apply prepositional phrases to their own work.

The final step is to ask students to look for ways to apply prepositional phrases to their own work. If students are currently working on a particular writing project, I recommend asking them to examine it for any sections of text that could benefit from additional detail and mark those examples. After they identify these sections, ask students to use some prepositional phrases to add appropriate details. I recommend conferencing with the

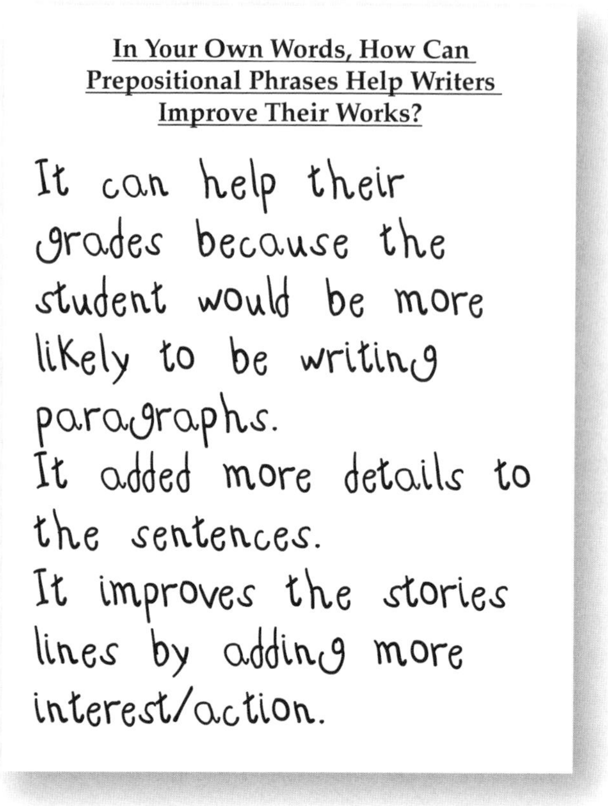

In Your Own Words, How Can Prepositional Phrases Help Writers Improve Their Works?

It can help their grades because the student would be more likely to be writing paragraphs.
It added more details to the sentences.
It improves the stories lines by adding more interest/action.

Figure 9.4 Reflection on Prepositional Phrases Activity

students while they do this so you can talk with them about which sections can benefit from extra detail and which prepositional phrases would be best included in those sections. Prepositional phrases can add detail to any genre of writing—short stories, poems, persuasive essays, and informational reports can all benefit from them.

Final Thoughts on Prepositional Phrases

The following information summarizes major points from this chapter, including what this grammatical concept is, why it's important for good writing, and how one might teach it for maximum effectiveness.

- ◆ Prepositional phrases are included in Common Core Language Standard 4.1.
- ◆ A prepositional phrase is a group of words that begins with a preposition and ends with a noun or pronoun, which is called the object of the preposition.
- ◆ Some common prepositions are *above, behind,* and *during.*
- ◆ Some prepositional phrases that feature those prepositions are above the ground, behind the car, and during the game.

◆ Writers use prepositional phrases to add details to their work.
◆ When teaching students about prepositional phrases, try these four things:
  • Show students how published authors use prepositional phrases.
  • Help students remove the prepositional phrases in published pieces and substitute new ones.
  • Have students add prepositional phrases to examples of "bland" writing.
  • Ask students to look for ways to apply prepositional phrases to their own work.

10

Guidelines for Capitalization Use

What Are the Guidelines for Capitalization Use?

Common Core Language Standard 4.2 addresses the importance of capitalization. The standard's overarching statement calls for students to "Demonstrate command of the conventions of standard English capitalization, punctuation, and spelling when writing," and its first subheading specifically states students need to "Use correct capitalization" (Common Core Standards, 2010).

Given the emphasis this standard places on capitalization, students need to master key guidelines for correct capitalization use. Although there are a number of rules about capital letters, this chapter focuses on some major ones that are likely to be relevant to the needs of fourth-grade writers:

- ♦ Capitalize the first letter of the first word in a sentence.
- ♦ Capitalize the pronoun *I*.
- ♦ Capitalize proper nouns—specific names of people, places, and things.
- ♦ Capitalize titles that come before names.
- ♦ Capitalize days of the week, months of the year, and holidays.
- ♦ Capitalize the names of countries, nationalities, and specific languages.

If students master these rules, they'll be on track for demonstrating command of standard English capitalization in their writing. Figure 10.1 (page 102) provides examples of these six capitalization rules.

Figure 10.1 Key Capitalization Rules and Examples

Rule	Example
1. Capitalize the first letter of the first word in a sentence.	**She** is going to play soccer today.
2. Capitalize the pronoun *I*.	**I** am going to play soccer with her.
3. Capitalize proper nouns.	Last summer, **I** visited the **Atlantic Ocean**. **Note:** If this sentence read "Last summer, I visited the ocean," *ocean* would not be capitalized because it doesn't name a specific ocean.
4. Capitalize titles that come before names.	I am going to speak with **Mayor Jones**. **Note:** If this sentence read, "I am going to speak with the mayor," *mayor* would not be capitalized because the title doesn't come before a name.
5. Capitalize days of the week, months of the year, and holidays.	**Halloween** is the final day of **October**.
6. Capitalize the names of countries, nationalities, and specific languages.	His family is from **Mexico**.

Why Capitalization Is Important to Good Writing

The capitalization rules are important to good writing for two main, related reasons: they provide clarity and enhance the reader's experience. A piece with correct capitalization gets the author's message across and doesn't distract or confuse readers. In this section, we'll look at each reason in more detail, using examples from published works for support.

Clarity

When writers follow capitalization rules, they ensure that their work makes sense. I like to use examples related to the capitalization of proper nouns to illustrate this to students. When discussing capitalization recently with a group of fourth graders, I showed them the following example from an article in *Sports Illustrated for Kids* about two professional basketball teams, the Miami Heat and Oklahoma City Thunder: "Oklahoma City was left wondering what changes it should make to beat the Heat in the future" (Repanich, 2012, p. 23). We discussed that *Heat* is capitalized in this sentence because it's a proper noun; it names a professional basketball team. If the article instead read *heat*, it would refer to warm temperatures, not the NBA team. Readers might think the article was talking about people in Oklahoma City trying to cool down from the warm temperature outside rather than one basketball team trying to defeat another.

Enhance Readers' Experience

Proper capitalization use helps readers enjoy a piece of writing without being distracted by mistakes. Capitalization mistakes result in readers spending more time deciphering the mistakes than enjoying the writing. In the following example from the mystery novel *It Happened on a Train*, author Mac Barnett used punctuation and capitalization to show where one sentence ends and another begins: "Steve's skin was starting to sting. His head throbbed" (Barnett, 2011, p. 150). If this passage instead read, "Steve's skin was starting to sting. **his** head throbbed," readers would probably be confused because **his** does not begin with a capital letter. They might wonder if the author meant to use this word to start a new sentence.

As these examples illustrate, correct capitalization helps a piece of writing make sense and maximizes readers' enjoyment of the work. Next, we'll look at Ms. Walker's classroom instruction and see how she helps her students master capitalization.

A Classroom Snapshot

On a cold, gray Tuesday morning, Ms. Walker's students appear ready to face the day. They've put away their coats and are seated at their desks, focused on the sentence Ms. Walker wrote on the board. Though it's possible that the students are just really excited about studying capitalization, a more likely explanation is that they're intrigued by the sentence from *Harry Potter and the Sorcerer's Stone*: "Harry clambered on to his Nimbus Two Thousand" (Rowling, 1997, p.185).

"Are we talking about Harry Potter today?" a student calls out excitedly.

"We're talking more about capitalization today," Ms. Walker replies, "but we'll use Harry Potter to get started."

Ms. Walker's class has been discussing capitalization, in connection with Common Core Language Standard 4.2, for the past few classes. They've talked about key capitalization rules, such as those listed in the beginning of this chapter, and looked at examples of each of them. In today's class, Ms. Walker hopes to use literature to engage her students in a discussion of capitalization. When I met with her before this lesson, she told me she wanted the students to consider *why* some words are capitalized, as this can help the students see how authors put capitalization rules into practice. Because she had used *Harry Potter and the Sorcerer's Stone* as a read aloud at the beginning of the school year and so many of her students had enjoyed it, Ms. Walker felt this would be a good text from which to choose some examples.

Now let's return to this lesson on capitalization. Ms. Walker asks a volunteer to read the sentence aloud. After a student does so, Ms. Walker explains that they're going to use this sentence, and some other examples from this book, to discuss capitalization. "We're going to talk about which words are capitalized and why J. K. Rowling capitalized them," she says. After stating this, Ms. Walker asks if any students can identify an example of capitalization in this sentence.

Hands fly up all over the classroom, and Ms. Walker calls on a student sitting toward the back of the room, who says, "The *h* in *Harry* is capitalized."

Ms. Walker follows up: "And *why* is the *h* in *Harry* capitalized?"

Students again raise their hands; Ms. Walker calls on a female student near the front of the class: "It's the first word [in the sentence], and it's a name."

"Those are two good reasons why it's capitalized," Ms. Walker explains. "Even if *Harry* wasn't the first word in the sentence, it still would start with a capital letter because it's someone's name. There are more capital letters in this sentence; can anyone tell us any of those?"

Hands once again sprout up; a student explains, "All the words in *Nimbus Two Thousand* are capitalized."

"Yes, all the first letters of all those words are capitalized," Ms. Walker states. "Why do you think that is?"

The same student replies, "*Nimbus Two Thousand* is the name of Harry's broom, so it's capitalized."

"And because it's the name of his broom, that makes it what?" Ms. Walker asks.

Several students call out, "A proper noun!"

"That's right," responds Ms. Walker. "*Nimbus Two Thousand* is a proper noun, so its first letters are capitalized." She motions to the sentence again and provides further explanation. "In this sentence, the first letter in *Harry* is capitalized because it begins the sentence and is someone's name. The first letters in the words *Nimbus Two Thousand* are all capitalized because that's the name of Harry's broom. We're going to work with one more sentence from *Harry Potter*," she says, smiling, as some students cheer.

Ms. Walker writes on the board, "Before Ron could answer, Professor Flitwick appeared at Malfoy's elbow" (Rowling, 1997, p.165) and explains that she is going to underline all the capitalized words and ask volunteers to explain why those words are capitalized. She says that, after the students share these reasons, she'll write those explanations under the words. Ms. Walker proceeds to underline *Before*, *Ron*, *Professor*, *Flitwick*, and *Malfoy*. She turns back to the class and asks, "Can anyone tell us why the first letter in *Before* is capitalized?"

A student raises her hand and explains, "Because it starts the sentence."

"Right," replies Ms. Walker; she writes the words *starts sentence* on the board underneath *Before*.

"How about *Ron*?" she asks. "Why is that capitalized?"

Another student volunteers: "It's capitalized because it's his name."

Ms. Walker nods and then writes *name* underneath the word *Ron*. "What about *Professor*? Why is that one capitalized?" she asks the class.

The students hesitate, so Ms. Walker takes this opportunity to remind them: "It's a job title that comes before a name. Kind of like Coach Smith," she says. "*Professor* is a job title and *Flitwick* is the professor's name. That's not always an easy thing to remember. You capitalize titles that come before names, just like this one." Ms. Walker proceeds to write *title* under the word *Professor* and *name* under *Flitwick*. "Now we have one more capitalized word: *Malfoy*!"

Students jokingly boo Harry Potter's nemesis, Draco Malfoy, while one smiles and says, "It's a name."

"Yes, a name," says Ms. Walker as she writes *name* under the word *Malfoy*. "Very nice job today," she says. "Everyone did a really good job saying why these words are capitalized. You're really getting these capitalization rules."

Recommendations for Teaching Students About Capitalization Use

In this section, I describe a step-by-step instructional process to use when teaching students about capitalization:

1. Show students examples from published texts and discuss the capitalization with them.
2. Give students examples of uncapitalized text and have them correct the examples.
3. Ask students to explain the corrections they made.
4. Have students focus on capitalization when editing and analyzing their own writing.

These instructional steps were designed to help students apply their knowledge of capitalization rules, so use the information at the beginning of this chapter to ensure that students understand the fundamentals of capitalization before beginning this process. The goal is to help students think about *why* writers use capitalization in the ways they do; reflecting on this topic can help students understand why capitalization is important to effective writing and help them correctly implement it in their own work.

1. Show students examples from published texts and discuss the capitalization with them.

Ms. Walker's work with her students in the Classroom Snapshot is an example of this step: she showed her students examples from *Harry Potter and the Sorcerer's Stone* (Rowling, 1997) and talked with them about why the first letters in certain words are capitalized. By explaining these reasons, the students were forced to apply their understanding of capitalization rules to a piece of writing because they needed to justify J. K. Rowling's decisions about capitalization based on their own knowledge of capitalization rules. This required the students to think analytically about capitalization in a way they wouldn't do if they were only memorizing the rules about this concept.

When conducting this activity with your students, I recommend selecting a high-interest text, as Ms. Walker did. After you do this, find a sentence from the text and display it prominently. Then ask for student volunteers to tell you the reason behind each example of capitalization. As students respond, monitor their insights and identify any capitalization rules with which they might need extra help. This activity can be a great opportunity for evaluating students' understanding and re-teaching certain aspects of capitalization. I recommend doing this activity twice, each time with sentences that contain different kinds of capitalized words: for example, one sentence might include only capitalized names of people; another might include more challenging capitalization rules to learn, such as days of the week and names of languages.

2. Give students examples of uncapitalized text and have them correct the examples.

After you discuss with students the capitalization in published works, I recommend giving them examples of text without any capitalization and asking them to rewrite the examples with appropriate capitalization. This activity can be done with examples from published texts with the capitalization removed or with sentences you create specifically for the activity. Either tactic can work well as long as the example is aligned with the capitalization rules you've discussed with your students. For example, if you've spent a lot of time talking about the importance of capitalizing the days of the week, try to give students an example with some days of the week in it. Below is an example I created that was geared toward the concepts I was focusing on in my instruction. I created this example because my students and I had spent a lot of time talking about the need to capitalize names of specific languages and holidays, and this passage contains examples of those things.

> **Passage I Showed Students**
> tomorrow, josé and his grandparents are going to celebrate thanksgiving at greg's house. greg's family speaks english and josé's grandparents speak spanish, but josé speaks both spanish and english, so he will translate.

Passage With Correct Capitalization
Tomorrow, José and his grandparents are going to celebrate Thanksgiving at Greg's house. Greg's family speaks English and José's grandparents speak Spanish, but José speaks both Spanish and English, so he will translate.

3. Ask students to explain the corrections they made.

Once students correct the uncapitalized examples you gave them, ask them to explain why they made those corrections. Asking students to justify their decisions helps them connect their corrections with their knowledge of the capitalization rules. To facilitate this, I create a T-chart on the board or a large sheet of paper with Capitalized Words on one side and Reasons on the other and ask students to copy this chart in their notebooks. On the Capitalized Words side, the students write the words they capitalized; on the Reasons side, they write why they chose to capitalize each of those words. After the students complete the activity individually, I ask volunteers to share their responses. As they share, I write their responses on the original T-chart I showed them at the beginning of the activity.

Figure 10.2 (below) depicts a chart that I filled out based on my students' responses to the passage about Thanksgiving. It contains the words they chose to capitalize and the reasons for their decisions.

Figure 10.2 Capitalized Words and Reasons

Capitalized Words	Reasons
Tomorrow	First word in sentence
José	Proper noun
Thanksgiving	Holiday
Greg	Proper noun
English	Language
Spanish	Language

4. Have students focus on capitalization when editing and analyzing their own writing.

Once students complete these activities and you're satisfied with their understanding of capitalization, have them apply this concept to their own writing. I recommend asking students to look at the capitalization in a piece of writing on which they're currently working. When I ask students to do this, I like to have them fill out a Capitalization Chart, displayed in Figure 10.3 (below). It asks students to note some examples of correct

Figure 10.3 Capitalization Chart

Use the chart below to list five capitalized words from your writing and the reason each word is capitalized.

Capitalized Words	Reasons

capitalization in their work and to reflect on why the examples of correct punctuation in their writing are correct. This activity requires students to analyze the capitalization present in their own writing. Access the supplemental downloads (see page iv) for a printable version of this chart.

Final Thoughts on Capitalization Use

The following information summarizes major points from this chapter, including what this grammatical concept is, why it's important for good writing, and how one might teach it for maximum effectiveness.

- ◆ Correct capitalization use is addressed in Common Core Language Standard 4.2.
- ◆ Here are six key guidelines for capitalization use especially relevant to fourth graders:
  - Capitalize the first letter of the first word in a sentence.
  - Capitalize the pronoun *I*.
  - Capitalize proper nouns—specific names of people, places, and things.
  - Capitalize titles that come before names—Mayor Jones.
  - Capitalize days of the week, months of the year, and holidays.
  - Capitalize the names of countries, nationalities, and specific languages.
- ◆ Capitalization is important for good writing because writing with correct capitalization gets the author's message across and doesn't distract or confuse readers.
- ◆ When teaching students about capitalization use, do these four things:
  - Show students examples from published texts and discuss the capitalization with them.
  - Give students examples of uncapitalized text and have them correct the examples.
  - Ask students to explain the corrections they made.
  - Have students focus on capitalization when editing and analyzing their own writing.

11

Choosing Words and Phrases to Convey Ideas Precisely

What Does "Choose Words and Phrases That Convey Ideas Precisely" Mean?

Common Core Language Standard 4.3 calls for students to "Use words and phrases to convey ideas precisely" as part of a more general statement that students should "Use knowledge of language and its conventions when writing, speaking, reading, or listening" (Common Core Standards, 2010). To further explore this standard, let's think about what "convey ideas precisely" mean. Sometimes people communicate in ways that are vague and general. In good writing, however, language that clearly expresses whatever the author wants to say and doesn't contain ambiguous and potentially confusing statements is important. In this chapter, we'll explore two language tools that writers use to convey their ideas clearly and precisely: specific nouns and strong verbs, which allow readers to picture specific images authors try to create (Robb, 2001).

Specific Nouns

Specific nouns in a piece of writing allow readers to clearly picture a particular person, place, or thing as the author envisions it (Robb, 2001). In contrast, vague or general nouns leave readers guessing. There are countless examples of specific nouns; to use them properly, a writer needs to think about what will most clearly communicate an idea or image to readers. For example, let's say I was talking about visiting a city and wanted to convey that I enjoyed looking at the buildings there. If I wrote, "I enjoyed looking at the buildings," readers would have a general idea of the situation but wouldn't know much about the kinds of buildings at which I looked.

Figure 11.1 General Nouns and Specific Noun Replacements

General Nouns	Specific Noun Replacements
sport	basketball football soccer tennis
building	skyscraper house grocery store mall
bird	cardinal vulture blue jay eagle

Buildings in this sentence is a vague noun; replacing it with a more specific one, such as *skyscrapers,* would provide a much more specific description of what I saw. Figure 11.1 (above) shows some examples of general nouns and some specific nouns that can replace them.

Strong Verbs

Just as specific nouns allow readers to picture particular people, places, or things, strong verbs allow readers to clearly imagine specific actions taking place (Robb, 2001). Robb explains that general (or weak) verbs allow a variety of interpretations, and strong verbs ensure that readers and the writer are thinking about the same action. For example, the verb *went* is considered weak because it is not specific. If I wrote, "Jim **went** outside," readers wouldn't know anything about how he went outside, which could be important information to the situation. Replacing *went* with a stronger verb, such as *trudged, charged,* or *sprinted,* would allow readers to clearly understand and envision Jim's actions in this situation. Figure 11.2 (page 113) shows some frequently used examples of weak verbs and some strong verbs that can replace them.

Why Conveying Ideas Precisely Is Important to Good Writing

Writers need to convey their ideas precisely; if they don't, their writing can be vague and hard to understand. Writers who use specific nouns and strong verbs can help readers clearly visualize what's taking place. For example, the sentence "I looked at a bird" gives readers some basic information but doesn't provide the same specific detail as "I stared at a hawk." Replacing *looked* with the strong verb *stared* and *bird* with the more specific

Figure 11.2 Weak Verbs and Strong Verb Replacements

Weak Verbs	Strong Verb Replacements
go	sprint trudge charge march
say	exclaim mumble whisper shout
throw	toss peg hurl chuck

noun *hawk* allows readers to clearly visualize what the author intended. In this section, we'll look at some published examples of specific nouns and strong verbs and talk about how the authors of those pieces use those tools to make their writing clear and specific.

Specific Nouns

In *Encyclopedia Brown and the Case of the Two Spies*, Donald J. Sobol used specific nouns to help readers clearly visualize situations, as in the following sentence: "Several little kids displayed their collections of trading cards, toys, bottle tops, marbles, and comic magazines" (Sobol, 1994, p. 53). To illustrate the importance of specific nouns to this sentence, let's look at how it would appear with vague, general nouns. Such a sentence might read, "Several people displayed their items." This sentence doesn't give readers the important details that Sobol's original work does; in the original sentence, specific nouns tell readers who performed the action and what was on display. The version with vague, general nouns leaves readers guessing about this information.

Another example of specific nouns from the same novel: "After hanging a garbage bag out of reach of raccoons, the boys tossed a football and explored the woods" (Sobol, 1994, p. 35). In this sentence, the specific nouns provide readers with information such as the kind of ball the boys tossed and the species of animal with which they were concerned. If the sentence read, "After hanging a garbage bag out of reach of *animals*, the boys tossed a *ball* and explored the woods," it would lack the specificity that makes the original example so strong. Picturing the action is much easier if readers know what type of animal the boys wanted to avoid and the kind of ball they were throwing.

Strong Verbs

In the book *Shipwreck*, Gordon Korman used strong verbs to clearly convey characters' actions. In the sentence "Luke Haggerty squeezed into the tiny bathroom and pulled the door shut behind him" (Korman, 2001, p. 3), Korman used the strong verb *squeezed* to help readers visualize Luke Haggerty's action. We can picture Luke struggling to enter the small bathroom and moving around uncomfortably while doing so. If the verb were weaker, such as *moved* or *went*, readers wouldn't be able to picture the action as clearly; the strong verb lets readers know exactly how this action was being performed.

Korman used another strong verb in the sentence". . . the flaming stump of the midmast toppled over in a shower of sparks" (Korman, 2001, p. 95). In the sentence, the verb *toppled* clearly indicates the way the midmast fell. If Korman used the more general verb *fell*, readers would not be able to envision the action as well. The strong verb *toppled* allows the reader to picture the action as Korman intended it.

These excerpts from Sobol's and Korman's novels illustrate the importance of clear writing. The specific nouns and strong verbs in these pieces allow readers to visualize what the authors intended. In the next section, we'll look at how Ms. Walker helps her students understand that specific nouns and strong verbs are tools for clear and effective writing.

A Classroom Snapshot

Ms. Walker knows a good thing when she sees it. In this case, the good thing is using *Harry Potter and the Sorcerer's Stone* to teach key grammatical concepts. Because her students responded well to examples from this novel in a lesson she recently conducted on capitalization, Ms. Walker is using it again in today's lesson on specific nouns and strong verbs. She begins the scheduled language arts time by pointing to a sentence she wrote on the whiteboard and reading it out loud: "As they jostled their way through a crowd of confused Hufflepuffs, Harry suddenly grabbed Ron's arm" (Rowling, 1977, p.173).

"This sentence is from *Harry Potter and the Sorcerer's Stone*," Ms. Walker says, as some students cheer. Smiling, she explains that they will refer to that sentence in today's discussion of specific nouns and strong verbs. Ms. Walker reminds the students of their previous conversations about specific nouns and strong verbs, asking them to look in their notebooks at examples they wrote down as part of those discussions. She asks volunteers to share examples of specific nouns and strong verbs. After a number of students volunteer this information, Ms. Walker explains how their previous work on this topic and today's class are related: "We've talked about what specific nouns and strong verbs are. Today, we're going to look at how a writer uses them."

"In *Harry Potter*!" a student interjects.

"Yes, in *Harry Potter*," Ms. Walker responds. "Look back at this sentence up here," she says as she gestures again toward the sentence on the board. "We're going to look at specific nouns and strong verbs in it. One specific noun in this sentence is *Hufflepuffs*," she declares as she underlines the word in the sentence. "Can anyone tell us why this is a specific noun?"

A female student raises her hand: "Hufflepuffs are students at Hogwarts."

Ms. Walker nods and replies, "*Hufflepuffs* refers to a specific group of students. Can anyone tell us a less specific word for *Hufflepuffs*?"

Another student raises his hand: "How about *students*?"

"Right," says Ms. Walker. "*Students* is less specific than *Hufflepuffs*. They're both correct, but *Hufflepuffs* tells us specifically what they are." She writes *students* underneath the word *Hufflepuffs*. Next, Ms. Walker turns the class's attention to strong verbs. "Now let's think about the strong verbs in this sentence. Remember that strong verbs clearly show readers exactly what someone or something does. A strong verb in this example is *jostled*. The word *jostle* means 'move in a rough way.' If someone is moving through a crowd, bumping into people, and pushing past them, the person is jostling. I try to make sure you don't jostle past one another when it's time for recess," she says with a smile as some students laugh. "*Jostle* is a strong verb because it tells us exactly how Harry and Ron were moving. Can anyone think of a weaker, or less specific, word for *jostled*?"

Students look around hesitantly; one volunteers a response: "*Moved*?"

"*Moved*," repeats Ms. Walker. "Jostling is a specific way of moving, so *moved* is a weaker verb that can replace *jostle*." She looks back at the sentence on the board, underlines "jostled their way," writes *moved* underneath it, and asks, "Remember yesterday when we talked about strong verbs that can replace *said* and talked about how you can use *yell* or *whisper* or many other words to show how someone said something?" A number of students nod; Ms. Walker continues: "*Jostled* is a word that tells us how Harry and Ron moved." More students nod, appearing to grasp the concept.

"Now," Ms. Walker says, "I'm going to rewrite this sentence with new words: a nonspecific noun and a weak verb." She writes, "As they moved through a crowd of confused students, Harry suddenly grabbed Ron's arm," next to the original version. Ms. Walker reads the new sentence out loud and asks the students, "What do you think is different about this new one?"

Students all over the room raise their hands; the boy Ms. Walker calls on explains: "This new one doesn't say as much. Like, it doesn't explain that the students are Hufflepuffs. It just says they're students. And it doesn't tell us Harry and Ron had to jostle through the crowd. It just says they moved."

"That's right," responds Ms. Walker, "and it's because this new version doesn't have all the specific nouns and strong verbs the original one does.

We'll be doing more work with specific nouns and strong verbs tomorrow. You're going to look through some books and pick these things out."

As the students nod, one says, "I had no idea these things were so important."

"Do you see why they are important?" Ms. Walker asks.

"Yeah, they make writing a lot better and a lot clearer."

Recommendations for Teaching Students About Specific Nouns and Strong Verbs

In this section, I describe a step-by-step instructional process to use when teaching students about specific nouns and strong verbs, grammatical concepts writers can use to convey their ideas clearly and precisely:

1. Show students examples of published works that contain specific nouns and strong verbs.
2. Have students change these examples and discuss the new meanings.
3. Ask students to find examples of specific nouns and strong verbs in literature.
4. Ask students to analyze why using these tools produces clear and specific writing.

Because these instructional steps are intended to be applications of students' knowledge of this concept, I recommend using the charts and descriptions at the beginning of this chapter to help students grasp the fundamentals of specific nouns and strong verbs before beginning these steps.

1. Show students examples of published works that contain specific nouns and strong verbs.

I recommend beginning these instructional steps by showing students examples of published works that contain specific nouns and strong verbs. This introduces students to ways professional writers use these tools to enhance the clarity of their writing. These published works provide the starting point for further discussion and analysis of these concepts that comes later. Ms. Walker selected one sentence from *Harry Potter and the Sorcerer's Stone* that contained a specific noun and a strong verb example. Though this method certainly works well, selecting a separate sentence to illustrate each concept can also be effective. Either tactic can provide students with strong examples of specific nouns and strong verbs.

2. Have students change these examples and discuss the new meanings.

After you show students examples of specific nouns and strong verbs in published writing, ask the students to replace them with general nouns and weak verbs. The point is to show students how much less effective a piece of writing becomes when it is no longer clear and specific. Identify some specific nouns and strong verbs in the examples, and then ask students for more general replacements for them. Once students have come up with these replacements, write the new version of the text next to the original one so students can clearly see the difference. When doing such an activity with a fourth-grade student, I showed him the following excerpt from Kathryn Lasky's novel *The Coming of Hoole*, from the Guardians of Ga'hoole series: "'Atta boy!' Grank boomed. Hoole shuddered and nearly dropped the worm" (Lasky, 2006, p. 7). A bit of explanation of this sentence: Grank and Hoole are owls; Grank is praising Hoole for catching a worm for the first time. I began a discussion of this sentence by pointing out the strong verb *boomed* and the specific noun *worm*. I asked the student to replace *boomed* with a weaker verb and *worm* with a less-specific noun. He replaced *boomed* with *said* and *worm* with *food* (since Hoole caught the worm in order to eat it), creating the new passage "'Atta boy!' Grank *said*. Hoole shuddered and nearly dropped the *food*." The student and I then discussed what information we learn from the original sentence that we don't learn from the new one. According to the student, without the strong verb *boomed* and the specific noun *worm*, "You don't know how Grank said what he said and you don't know what the food is."

3. Ask students to find examples of specific nouns and strong verbs in literature.

Once students have discussed specific nouns and strong verbs with you, they're ready to find them on their own! Asking students to find examples of specific nouns and strong verbs in literature requires them to keep these grammatical concepts in mind while they read. To get students going on this activity, ask them to choose a book from your classroom library and tell them they'll be looking at how the author of that work used strong verbs and specific nouns to make the information in the book as clear and specific as possible. I recommend giving students post-it notes to mark strong verbs and specific nouns they find. I instruct my students to write *N* on each post-it note they use to mark a specific noun and *V* on each one they use to mark a strong verb. This way, their findings are clearly identified, and they can track how many of each they've located.

4. Ask students to analyze why using these tools produces clear and specific writing.

Finally, I recommend asking students to analyze why the specific nouns and strong verbs they located in their books make the writing clear and specific. To help them do this, I give them two charts: a Specific Noun Analysis Chart, Figure 11.3, and a Strong Verb Analysis Chart, Figure 11.4 (page 118). (Blank, printable versions of these charts are available for download. See page iv.)

Figure 11.3 Model of Analysis Chart One: Specific Noun Analysis

Specific Noun From the Book You Used	Less-Specific Noun That Could Replace It	Why Using Specific Nouns Produces Better Writing
worm	food	"Worm" tells the reader specifically what kind of food Hoole caught. If the author said "food," readers wouldn't know what he caught, only that he caught something to eat.

Figure 11.4 Model of Analysis Chart Two: Strong Verb Analysis

Strong Verb From the Book You Used	Weak Verb That Could Replace It	Why Using Strong Verbs Produces Better Writing
boomed	said	"Boomed" shows the reader exactly how Grank spoke. It creates a much more specific mental image than "said."

These charts ask students to identify some specific nouns and strong verbs in the books they used, come up with less-specific examples, and reflect on why the original text is better than the less-specific one. Completing these charts draws from all the steps of this instructional process and asks students to use the skills they developed during these activities.

Before students get started, it's a good idea to model for them how to complete each of these charts. To do this, think back to the example you discussed with your students. If you have a document projector, place the Specific Noun Analysis Chart on it and write down a specific noun from the sentence you and the class discussed. Then write the general noun your students suggested replacing it with, and write a brief analysis of why using the specific version produces better writing. Do the same with the Strong Verb Analysis Chart, using a strong verb you and the class discussed and replaced during the same activity. This shows the students exactly what's expected of them and provides them with support that will help them complete the task on their own. For example, you could model this activity using the sentences "'Atta boy!' Grank boomed. Hoole shuddered and nearly dropped the worm" (Lasky, 2006, p. 7) previously discussed in this chapter, and the replacement words used by the student with whom I worked. To do so, you could display the model charts in Figures 11.3 and 11.4 (page 118), which identify specific nouns and strong verbs in these sentences and explain their benefits.

Once students get started working on their own, I like to move around the room and check in with them so that I can see the words they're identifying and the reflections they're composing. It's rewarding to observe students engaging in metacognitive analysis of these grammatical concepts!

Final Thoughts on Choosing Words and Phrases to Convey Ideas Precisely

The following information summarizes major points from this chapter, including what this grammatical concept is, why it's important for good writing, and how one might teach it for maximum effectiveness.

- ◆ Common Core Language Standard 4.3 calls for students to "Use words and phrases to convey ideas precisely" (Common Core Standards, 2010).
- ◆ It's important that writers use language that clearly expresses what they want to say and doesn't contain ambiguous and potentially confusing statements.
- ◆ Two language tools that writers use to convey their ideas clearly and precisely are specific nouns and strong verbs.
  - Specific nouns in a piece of writing allow readers to clearly picture a particular person, place, or thing. For example, *hawk* is a specific noun; *bird* is a general one.
  - Strong verbs allow readers to clearly imagine specific actions taking place. For example, *sprinted* is a strong verb; *went* is a weak one.
- ◆ When teaching specific nouns and strong verbs, try these four things:
  - Show students examples of published works that contain specific nouns and strong verbs.
  - Have students change these examples and discuss the new meanings.
  - Ask students to find examples of specific nouns and strong verbs in literature.
  - Ask students to analyze why using these tools produces clear and specific writing.

Section 3

Grammatical Concepts Aligned With Grade Five Common Core Language Standards

12

The Perfect Verb Tenses

What Are the Perfect Verb Tenses?

Common Core Language Standard 5.1 addresses the perfect verb tenses, calling for students to "Form and use the perfect (e.g., *I had walked*; *I have walked*; *I will have walked*) verb tenses" (Common Core Standards, 2010) as part of a more general statement that students should show command of grammatical conventions. There are three perfect verb tenses: the past perfect, the present perfect, and the future perfect. Each tense refers to a completed action (the word *perfect*, in this sense, is a synonym for *completed*). Let's look at each perfect tense in more detail.

The Past Perfect
The past perfect tense is formed by combining *had* with the past participle of a verb, creating combinations such as "had read." It describes an action that was completed in the past before another past action took place, such as in the following example: "Kate **had read** the book before she saw the movie." In this example, two events occurred in the past: Kate read the book, and Kate saw the movie. "Had read" is in the past perfect tense because it explains that she finished reading the book before seeing the movie.

The Present Perfect
The present perfect tense is formed by combining *has* or *have* with the past participle of a verb, creating combinations such as "has finished." This tense describes an action that happened at an unspecified time in the past and has some relevance to the present, such as "Ben **has finished** his homework."

Figure 12.1 The Perfect Verb Tenses

Tense	What It Does	What It Looks Like	How It's Formed
Past Perfect	Describes an action that was completed in the past before another past action took place	Freddie **had washed** the dishes before he ate dessert.	Combine *had* with the past participle of a verb.
Present Perfect	Describes an action that happened at an unspecified time in the past and has some relevance to the present	Mimi **has eaten** her dessert and is now watching a movie.	Combine *has* or *have* with the past participle of a verb.
Future Perfect	Describes an action that will be completed in the future before another future action occurs	Mimi **will have seen** the movie before her parents do.	Combine *will* and *have* with the past participle of a verb.

Sentences in the present perfect tense often explain how the completed action relates to the current situation, such as "Ben **has finished** his homework and now is playing a video game." This sentence suggests that Ben is currently playing a video because he has completed his homework.

The Future Perfect

The future perfect tense is formed by combining *will* and *have* with the past participle of a verb, creating combinations such as "will have finished." This tense describes an action that will be completed in the future before another future action occurs. For example, the sentence "I **will have finished** my dinner before Jake arrives" is an example of the future perfect tense. It tells readers that the speaker will complete the act of eating dinner before another event occurs—in this case, the arrival of another person.

Figure 12.1 (above) summarizes some key points regarding the past, present, and future verb tenses.

A Note on Past Participles

The past, present, and future perfect tenses are all formed using the past participles of verbs. The past participle of a regular verb is formed by adding –*ed* to the end of the verb. The past participles of irregular verbs vary and are not governed by specific rules or patterns. Figure 12.2 (page 125) contains the past participles of some common irregular verbs.

Figure 12.2 Past Participles of Some Common Irregular Verbs

Base Form of Verb	Past Participle
be	been
have	has
do	done
say	said
make	made

Why the Perfect Verb Tenses Are Important to Good Writing

The perfect verb tenses are important tools for good writing because they allow writers to describe completed actions in clear and specific detail. These tenses allow writers to express whether an action was completed in the past before another past action took place (past perfect), whether an action was completed in the past and is relevant to the present (present perfect), or whether an action will be completed in the future before another future action occurs (future perfect). Without the perfect verb tenses, writers wouldn't be able to describe completed actions with this much specificity, and the clarity of their writing might suffer.

In the book *Pippi Longstocking*, author Astrid Lindgren used perfect verb tenses to clearly express the circumstances around important events. For example, she used the present perfect tense in a conversation between Pippi and two police officers. Upon meeting Pippi, one officer asks the other, "Is this the girl who **has moved** into Villa Villekula?" (Lindgren, 1950, p. 39). The present perfect (has moved) was used here because Pippi's move to Villa Villekula (an old house, formerly owned by Pippi's now-deceased father, in which she now lives by herself) happened at an unspecified time in the past and is relevant to the present. Pippi's residence there is relevant to the present because town officials are attempting to have her removed from this house and sent to live in a children's home. Pippi, showing her trademark wit, replies, "I am a child and this is my home: therefore it is a children's home" (Lindgren, 1950, p.40).

Lindgren used the past perfect tense in the following example, which describes a series of events at Pippi's birthday party: "When Mr. Nilsson **had emptied** his cup he turned it upside down and put it on his head" (Lindgren, 1950, p. 151). The past perfect (had emptied) clearly indicates that a past action (Mr. Nilsson, Pippi's pet monkey, emptying his cup) was completed before another action took place (Mr. Nilsson's turning the cup upside down and putting it on his head). Lindgren again used the past perfect in the sentence "When everybody **had had** enough and the horse **had**

had his share, Pippi took hold of all four corners of the tablecloth and lifted it up so that the cups and plates tumbled over each other as if they were in a sack" (Lindgren, 1950, p. 152). In this sentence, which also describes events of Pippi's birthday party, the author used the past perfect (had had) twice to indicate that "everyone **had had** enough and the horse **had had** his share" before Pippi folded up the tablecloth.

As these examples from *Pippi Longstocking* show, writers can use the perfect verb tenses to describe the circumstances around completed actions. Astrid Lindgren used the present perfect (**has moved**) to describe a completed action that is relevant to a current situation and the past perfect (**had emptied** and **had had**) to indicate completed actions that took place before another past action occurred. The perfect verb tenses allow writers to clearly express these distinctions, making them important grammatical tools. In the next section, we'll see how a fifth-grade teacher, Ms. Fernandez, helps her students understand these tenses.

A Classroom Snapshot

I enter Ms. Fernandez's fifth grade classroom and see a PowerPoint presentation projected on the screen at the front of the room. The title slide reads, The Perfect Verb Tenses. I sit down at a small table in the back of the classroom and wait for the language arts period to begin. For the past two classes, Ms. Fernandez and her students have been focusing on the perfect verb tenses as part of a school-wide focus on the Common Core Language Standards. They've discussed what the past, present, and future verb tenses are, looked at examples of each, and discussed the differences in the meanings of each of these tenses. Today they'll be working in groups to apply their knowledge of the perfect verb tenses.

When I first met with Ms. Fernandez, a relatively new teacher in her third year in the classroom, two week prior to this lesson, she shared with me her background on grammar instruction: "I think I know grammar well, but I learned it through textbooks, work sheets, and tests. We diagrammed a lot of sentences and definitely didn't do group work or talk about grammar as a tool for writing." I nodded, understanding the situation. Many people believe they should teach using the methods their teachers used (Mayher, 1990), although research indicates that grammar instruction taught out of context from student writing, such as the kind Ms. Fernandez experienced as a student, lowers student engagement (Woltjer, 1998) and doesn't do much to improve student writing (Weaver, 1998). Although Ms. Fernandez said she would feel most comfortable teaching grammar with a textbook and work sheets, she explained that she was open to trying a more interactive approach that connects grammatical concepts with writing instruction: "I'm most comfortable with teaching the way I was taught, but I want to teach in the way that will most help my students."

In today's language arts period, Ms. Fernandez will engage her students in a group activity related to the past, present, and future verb tenses. She begins the class by reminding her students that they've been discussing the three perfect verb tenses and then asking for a student volunteer to remind the class of all three of these tenses.

"Past perfect, present perfect, and future perfect," replies a student.

"Excellent," responds Ms. Fernandez. "Take a look at the PowerPoint so we can review some examples of those tenses." Ms. Fernandez takes the students through three PowerPoint slides, each one with an example of one of the perfect verb tenses on it. She shows students each of these examples, asks volunteers to identify the tenses, and reviews the different meanings of each of the tenses. After this, Ms. Fernandez shows the students a slide containing a past tense sentence: "I listened to my favorite song." She asks the class, "Is this verb in one of the perfect tenses?" she asks.

"No," replies a student. "That's not one of them. That's just the past tense."

"Correct. This is in the past tense," responds Ms. Fernandez. "In your table groups [the 25 students in the class sit at five tables of five students each], work together and change the verb in this sentence to the past perfect, present perfect, and future perfect tenses. I'm going to give each group a marker and a large piece of paper, and then you can get started. Write each of your new sentences on the piece of paper I give you. Also write which tense each verb is in."

Ms. Fernandez takes a box of markers and a large easel pad from behind her desk and walks around the room. As she comes to each table, she tears off a piece of paper from the easel pad and gives the group's members a marker from the box. As the students work, they raise their hands with various questions, and Ms. Fernandez darts from group to group assisting the students. One group is having a particularly hard time with the past perfect tense. "Remember, in the past perfect, we use *had* and the past participle of the verb, such as *had watched* or *had gone*." The students nod. "That's right," says one. "I remember now."

"Can you put *listened*," Ms. Fernandez says to the group as she motions toward the sentence on the PowerPoint slide, "into the past perfect?"

Another student in the group responds. "Had listened," she says.

"Exactly!" replies Ms. Fernandez. "So, to make that a full sentence, you can say, 'I had listened to my favorite song when . . .' and then say something else that happened."

"OK, I get it," states one student, and the students in the group work together to complete this sentence. Ms. Fernandez listens to their discussion and then checks on the other groups. All groups appear to be done, so Ms. Fernandez asks each of them to share.

All five groups share, presenting their sentences to the class by posting their chart paper in the front of the room and reading the sentences they created. Ms. Fernandez remarks that one of the most interesting things about the students' sentences is the variation among them. For example, one group's present perfect sentence is "I have listened to my favorite song five times already today," another's is "I have listened to my favorite song so many times that I have it memorized," and yet another's is "I have listened to my favorite song on my iPod, so you can listen now if you want to." Ms. Fernandez praises this variation, telling the students, "You did a great job adding extra information" (by including details about listening to one's favorite song). Ms. Fernandez continues, "You made the sentences your own while also using the perfect tenses."

When I talked with Ms. Fernandez later in the week, she compared the group work and analysis of the perfect verb tenses with the traditional grammar book activities she had used as a student. "I think they could memorize these tenses if we used a textbook and work sheets and that sort of thing, but by creating these sentences in groups and talking about what the perfect verb tenses mean and why [one would] use them, their understanding is a lot better than if they memorized things." During this conversation, Ms. Fernandez also stated that she'd like to try incorporating examples from literature into her grammar instruction. She puts that idea into practice in upcoming classroom snapshots.

Recommendations for Teaching Students About Perfect Verb Tenses

In this section, I describe a step-by-step instructional process to use when teaching students about the past, present, and future perfect verb tenses:

1. Have students create and share examples of each perfect verb tense.
2. Ask students to compare the different meanings of the examples they created.
3. Ask students to look for the perfect verb tenses while they read literature.
4. Discuss with students why writers use the perfect verb tenses.

These instructional steps are best covered over multiple class periods, as this will allow teachers to discuss each component in depth and make sure students understand the fundamentals of the concept before they try to apply their knowledge. Because these steps were designed to be applications of the students' knowledge of the perfect verb tenses, I recommend beginning a study of these tenses by discussing the definition of each tense, showing students examples of each tense, and talking with students about how to form each tense. The charts and explanations at the beginning of this chapter are useful for helping students grasp the fundamentals of this concept.

1. Have students create and share examples of each perfect verb tense.

I recommend beginning this application of students' knowledge of the perfect verb tenses by asking them to work together to create examples.

I suggest opening the activity as Ms. Fernandez did, by showing students a sentence in a basic tense (such as the past, present, or future) and asking them to rewrite that sentence in each of the perfect tenses. This allows students to get hands-on experience creating examples of these tenses and provides a structured situation in which you can monitor their understanding.

As Ms. Fernandez did with her class, check in with the student groups and gauge their progress. Though there are times when you'll offer your support, remember that one benefit of students working collaboratively is that they can learn from one another. Once students finish creating their sentences and you're satisfied with their progress, ask each group to share its examples with the class. Students often enjoy seeing how their examples are similar to and different from those their classmates created. Recall Ms. Fernandez's students' present perfect examples; the various sentences they created using *have listened* shows the wide range of situations in which one might use this verb tense.

2. Ask students to compare the different meanings of the examples they created.

After students share their responses, and you note similarities and differences in the different sentences the student groups created, ask the students to examine their sentences again. This time, they'll be focusing on the meanings of the sentences they created and comparing the different meanings of those sentences. Though all the perfect verb tenses describe completed actions, they do so very differently. Asking students to compare the meanings of the sentences helps them comprehend that each verb tense has a distinct meaning that an author would use for a particular purpose.

When I recently worked with a fifth-grade class on this activity, one group shared the following sentences—all adaptations of the sentence "The show ended."

Past perfect:	"By the time we got there, the show had ended."
Present perfect:	"The show has ended, and now it's time to eat."
Future perfect:	"The show will have ended before you get here."

When I asked the students to compare these sentences, they called attention to the way all of the sentences deal with the same topic (the show ending) but give different kinds of information about it. For example, one student explained, "All of them [the sentences] talk about the show ending, but they say different things about it ending and why [the show ending] is important." As this student's comment indicates, the show's ending is significant to each of these sentences, but for different reasons.

3. Ask students to look for the perfect verb tenses while they read literature.

When the students have created their own examples and compared the meanings, ask them to look for examples of the perfect verb tenses while they read literature. When I do this with students, I ask them to look

Figure 12.3 Reading With the Perfect Verb Tenses in Mind

Book Title: *Throwing Smoke*		Author: Bruce Brooks
Sentence Containing a Perfect Verb Tense	**Past, Present, or Future Perfect Tense?**	**Signal Words**
"Delancey **had already run** in and picked up two bats, which she whirled around a couple of times before dropping one and standing up to the plate" (Brooks, 2000, p. 35).	Past perfect	Had already run
"The shortstop **had heard** Wren's comment" (Brooks, 2000, p. 73).	Past perfect	Had heard

Access the supplemental downloads for a blank template of this chart that you can copy for classroom use (see page iv).

through books from the classroom library and write down any examples of the perfect verb tenses they notice. Because not all books use the perfect verb tenses, I like to select some texts beforehand and mark chapters or sections that contain them with post-it notes. Figure 12.3 (above) is an example of a chart I use to model this activity. The column on the left asks for the sentence that contains an example of one of these tenses, the center column asks students to identify which of the perfect tenses it is, and the column on the right asks students to write the signal words that indicate which tense the sentence contains.

This activity helps increase students' awareness of the perfect verb tenses and shows them that these are tools writers use. If finding examples of the perfect verb tenses in the books you have access to is difficult, you can create your own examples of passages that contain one or more of the perfect tenses and ask students to identify them. If possible, though, I recommend asking students to look for perfect verb tenses in literature, as seeing grammatical concepts in published texts can help students grasp their importance and see them as tools professional writers use.

4. Discuss with students why writers use the perfect verb tenses.

Finally, I recommend talking with students about why writers use the perfect verb tenses. I like to have a "think-pair-share" (Lyman, 1987) conversation in which I pose a question and ask the students to reflect on it, discuss their ideas with a partner, and then share their responses with the whole class. When recently working with students on this topic, I wrote on the board, "Why do writers use the perfect verb tenses?" The students reflected on this question, jotted down some notes, and then shared their ideas with partners.

After about two minutes of partner conversation, I asked volunteers to share their ideas. One student explained, "Writers use the perfect verb tenses because they tell you more than the other ones do, like how the past perfect tense tells you that one thing happened before another." Another student response focused specifically on the future perfect verb tenses; when this student shared what she and her partner had discussed, she stated, "We talked a lot about the future perfect. Writers use it because there's no other tense that says the same thing. If you wanted to say, 'By next September, we will have started middle school,' you have to use that tense." These responses indicated to me that the students understood the specific reasons writers use the perfect verb tenses and saw them as tools good writers use in particular situations.

Final Thoughts on the Perfect Verb Tenses

The following information summarizes major points from this chapter, including what this grammatical concept is, why it's important for good writing, and how one might teach it for maximum effectiveness.

- ◆ The perfect verb tenses are included in Common Core Language Standard 5.1.
- ◆ There are three perfect verb tenses: the past perfect, present perfect, and future perfect.
- ◆ All the perfect verb tenses describe completed actions.
    - • The past perfect tense describes an action that was completed in the past before another past action took place.
    - • The present perfect tense describes an action that happened at an unspecified time in the past and has some relevance to the present.
    - • The future perfect tense describes an action that will be completed in the future before another future action occurs.
- ◆ The perfect verb tenses are important to good writing because they allow writers to describe completed actions in clear and specific detail.
- ◆ When teaching the perfect verb tenses, try these things:
    - • Have students create and share examples of each of the perfect verb tenses.
    - • Ask students to compare the different meanings of the examples they created.
    - • Ask students to look for the perfect verb tenses while they read literature.
    - • Discuss with students why writers use the perfect verb tenses.

13

Conjunctions and Interjections

What Are Conjunctions and Interjections?

Common Core Language Standard 5.1 calls for students to "Explain the function of conjunctions, prepositions, and interjections in general and their function in particular sentences" (Common Core Standards, 2010), as part of a more general statement about mastering conventions of standard English grammar. This chapter focuses on information about conjunctions and interjections (prepositions and prepositional phrases are discussed in chapter 9). Conjunctions and interjections have some key similarities, as both consist of very few words and can have a significant impact on a piece of writing. However, the particular impact each has is different: conjunctions link statements together and can combine shorter sentences to form longer ones; interjections express emotion to enhance a piece's effect on readers. Let's look at each concept separately and in more detail.

Conjunctions

There are three types of conjunctions: coordinating, subordinating, and correlative. All link statements together but in different ways and for different purposes. In the following sub-sections, we'll look at examples of these types of conjunctions and discuss how each one is used.

Coordinating conjunctions. The coordinating conjunctions combine statements of equal importance. Some high-frequency coordinating conjunctions are *for*, *and*, *nor*, *but*, *or*, *yet*, and *so*. For example, in the sentence "Catherine ate dinner **and** checked her email," the coordinating conjunction *and* combines information about Catherine's actions. Without this conjunction, the text would read, "Catherine ate dinner. She checked her

Figure 13.1 Conjunctions

Grammatical Concept	What It Is	Examples	Used in a Sentence
Coordinating conjunction	A word used to combine related statements of equal importance	for, and, nor, but, or, yet, so	Bob came to dinner, **but** Diane stayed home.
Correlative conjunction	A two-part structure used to connect two related statements of equal importance.	both-and, not only-but also, either-or, neither-nor	**Either** I will finish the project today, **or** I will finish it tomorrow.
Subordinating conjunction	A word or phrase used to link two statements when one is dependent on the other.	after, because, before, since, though, until, when, while	**Because** this is your first day here, I will give you some advice.

e-mail," creating sentences that are much choppier than the version with a coordinating conjunction.

Correlative conjunctions. The correlative conjunctions are two-part structures used to connect two related statements. Like the coordinating conjunctions, correlative conjunctions link two ideas of equal importance. Some common correlative conjunctions are *both-and*, *not only-but also*, *either-or*, and *neither-nor*. A sentence that includes correlative conjunctions typically begins with the first part of the conjunction; the second part appears toward the middle, as in "**Either** Joe will coach the baseball team **or** Bob will." In this sentence, *either* and *or* are correlative conjunctions; they allow the author to link these two statements about possible coaches for a baseball team in a single sentence.

Subordinating conjunctions. Coordinating and correlative conjunctions combine statements of equal importance; a subordinating conjunction links two statements when one is dependent on the other, such as "Because he is running in today's race, Steve is wearing his lucky sneakers." In this statement, *Because* is a subordinating conjunction; it links two statements and shows that one is dependent on the other. "Because he is running in today's race" could not exist on its own, but "Steve is wearing his lucky sneakers" could function independently as a sentence. Some common subordinating conjunctions are *after*, *because*, *before*, *since*, *though*, *until*, *when*, and *while*.

Figure 13.1 (page 134) summarizes some key points about conjunctions.

Interjections

Like conjunctions, interjections are single words or short phrases. However, interjections do not link statements together as conjunctions do; instead, they express emotion. Interjections usually are found at the beginnings of sentences, such as "Wow, I can't believe it." In this sentence, *wow* is an interjection used to express the emotion of surprise. Commas or exclamation points typically follow interjections. For example, the preceding sentence could be written as "Wow! I can't believe it." Though many interjections are single words, some are also short phrases used to express emotion, such as "Oh my!" and "No way!" Figure 13.2 (below) highlights some key points about interjections.

Why Conjunctions and Interjections Are Important to Good Writing

Conjunctions and interjections are important tools that writers use to enhance their works; although they play different roles in sentences, both consist of single words or short phrases that can dramatically impact a piece of writing. In this section, we'll look at some examples of published texts that include conjunctions and interjections. In addition, we'll consider how these grammatical concepts impact the sentences in which they are used.

Conjunctions

A written work without conjunctions would likely consist of a number of short, choppy sentences; conjunctions allow writers to combine these sentences and create smooth, easy-to-read pieces. In the following excerpt

Figure 13.2 Interjections

Grammatical Concept	Interjections
What are they?	Single words or short phrases used to express emotion.
What are some examples?	Some examples of single-word interjections are *wow*, *oh*, and *great*. Some examples of short phrase interjections are "my gosh," "no way," and "my word."
What do they look like in writing?	**Oh**, I didn't see you there. **No way!** We're in the same class!

from *Radio Fifth Grade*, Gordon Korman used the coordinating conjunction *and* to link two related statements: "Ms. Panagopoulos adjusted her huge glasses and smiled brightly at her class," (Korman, 1989, p. 27). Rewritten without *and*, the sentence could read, "Ms. Panagopoulous adjusted her huge glasses. She smiled brightly at her class." The revision created two short and choppy sentences instead of the one longer one Korman wrote.

In *Radio Fifth Grade*, Korman also used subordinating conjunctions to link statements in which one is dependent on the other, such as "**As** he and Brad took their desks, Benjy could see that the fight was resuming in the control room" (Korman, 1989, p. 27). In this sentence, *as* is the subordinating conjunction. The section of the sentence in which it appears ("As he and Brad took their desks") cannot stand by itself as a sentence. The subordinating conjunction *as* allows the author to combine these two statements and show the relationship between them.

Another example of a subordinating conjunction in this novel occurs in this sentence: "**While** Benjy, Ellen-Louise, and Arthur started work on their scripts, Mark got permission from Mr. Sword to go to the office and post the new 'Kidsview' sign-up sheet" (Korman, 1989, p. 18). In this example, *while* is the subordinating conjunction; as in the previous example, it links two statements by showing a relationship between them. By using the subordinating conjunction *while*, Korman can connect the statement about Benjy, Ellen-Louise, and Arthur with the one about Mark, showing that they took place at the same time.

Interjections

Interjections are important to good writing because they allow authors (and the characters they create) to express emotion. Interjections are often used in dialogue when an author wants to show a character being especially emotional. For example, in *Radio Fifth Grade*, a variety of interjections occur in the conversations between the book's characters, such as the following comment, in which Mr. Whitehead, the owner of a pet store, responds to a creative marketing idea: "'Of course!' exclaimed Mr. Whitehead. 'We've got a real winner here'" (Korman, 1989, p. 63). In this example, Mr. Whitehead's use of the interjection *of course* reveals his enthusiasm for the idea. If Mr. Whitehead did not use this interjection and said only, "We've got a real winner here," his statement wouldn't have the same enthusiasm.

A similar sentence in *Radio Fifth Grade* takes place in Mr. Whitehead's pet shop when a woman looks at a parrot in the store and says, "Gosh, you're beautiful!" (Korman, 1989, p. 63). The interjection *gosh* is important to this sentence; it lets readers know how strongly the speaker feels. This interjection clearly conveys the woman's strong reaction, producing an emotionally charged sentence.

In the next section, we'll look at how Ms. Fernandez helps her fifth graders understand the importance of conjunctions and interjections to good writing.

A Classroom Snapshot

When I enter Ms. Fernandez's classroom today, I notice a spring in her step. She smiles, greets me, and enthusiastically explains the day's plan: "We've discussed the basics of conjunctions and interjections. Right now, we're going to look at some examples of interjections and conjunctions from *Walk Two Moons* and then create new sentences without those words to show the differences." I smile back, excited for the lesson and happy that Ms. Fernandez has embraced this method of teaching grammar; despite her comfort with textbooks and traditional grammar workbook exercises, she's using literature to help her students see grammatical concepts as important tools for good writing. I sit down and take out my notepad, excited for what I'm going to see.

"Take a look up here, everyone," Ms. Fernandez says, waving her arm at the screen at the front of the room on which a PowerPoint slide is projected. The slide shows the following sentence from Sharon Creech's novel *Walk Two Moons*: "Ben tripped over the curb, and Mary Lou gave me a peculiar look" (Creech, 1994, p. 136). "You might remember this sentence from *Walk Two Moons*," she states; the class read this book earlier in the school year. Several students nod, while others continue to look intently at Ms. Fernandez and the board. Ms. Fernandez explains that a good way to study grammar can be to look at how professional authors use grammar in the pieces they write. "Sharon Creech is an outstanding writer," Ms. Fernandez states, "and we can use her writing to study conjunctions and interjections. This sentence here has a conjunction. Can anyone find it?"

A number of students raise their hands; Ms. Fernandez calls on a student who says, "It's *and*."

"Correct," replies Ms. Fernandez. "Who can tell us what kind of conjunction *and* is?"

Another student raises her hand and states, "A coordinating conjunction."

"Absolutely right," responds Ms. Fernandez. "*And* is one of the coordinating conjunctions. If we didn't have coordinating conjunctions, sentences like this one would have to be divided up into shorter ones." Ms. Fernandez pushes a button on her computer to reveal a new slide, which says, "Ben tripped over the curb. Mary Lou gave me a peculiar look."

"Here's the same sentence without the conjunction," Ms. Fernandez says. "When I got rid of the conjunction, I needed to turn this into two sentences. Why, do you think, did the author of this book choose to use a conjunction instead of writing it like this?"

The students pause for a moment, but then about half of them raise their hands. Ms. Fernandez calls on a student in the back left corner of the room, who states, "I think it's because it sounds better to say this in one sentence. Saying it in two sentences doesn't sound as good."

"Excellent," states Ms. Fernandez. "If these sentences were divided in two, they wouldn't sound as well-written because they'd be so short and chopped up. Now that we've talked about an example of a sentence from *Walk Two Moons* that includes a conjunction, let's talk about a sentence that has an interjection."

Ms. Fernandez changes the PowerPoint slide to a new one, which contains the following passage from *Walk Two Moons*:

"Do you want to hear about the lunatic?"
"Goodness!" Gram said, "as long as it's not too bloody" (Creech, 1994, p. 52).

"Look at this conversation from *Walk Two Moons*," Ms. Fernandez says. "Can anyone find an interjection?"

Student hands go up around the classroom; Ms. Fernandez scans the class and calls on a student at one of the front tables, who states, "*Goodness* is the interjection."

"Correct," responds Ms. Fernandez. "*Goodness* is an example of an interjection. Gram says it to show emotion. Let's look at the passage without this interjection."

Ms. Fernandez reveals a new PowerPoint slide, which contains the same text, with one exception: it no longer contains the interjection *goodness*:

"Do you want to hear about the lunatic?"
Gram said, "As long as it's not too bloody."

Ms. Fernandez asks the students how they think this one is different from the original example. "It's mostly the same," a young lady responds, "but Gram doesn't have as much feeling."

"Excellent," replies Ms. Fernandez. "Using the interjection *goodness* expresses additional feeling and emotion. Now I'd like each of you to take out your independent reading book and look for a sentence that contains an interjection and one that contains a conjunction. Once you find these, write them down in your response journals."

In the next day's language arts period, Ms. Fernandez plans to ask the students to remove the conjunctions and interjections from the sentences they found. After this, they will analyze what makes the sentences different and why the authors used those grammatical concepts. "I'm looking forward to hearing what they say," she tells me after class. "I really like how they're analyzing grammar this way."

Recommendations for Teaching Students About Conjunctions and Interjections

In this section, I describe a step-by-step instructional process to use when teaching students about conjunctions and interjections:

1. Show students examples of conjunctions and interjections from literature.

2. Remove the conjunctions and interjections and discuss the changed sentences.
3. Have students add conjunctions and interjections to basic sentences and reflect on the differences.
4. Ask students to look for places to add conjunctions and interjections to their writing.

I suggest spreading these steps over multiple class periods so that students can take their time with each step, and you can evaluate how well they understand one activity before moving on to the next. Because these steps are intended to be an application of students' understandings of conjunctions and interjections, use the tables and other information at the beginning of this chapter to discuss the fundamentals of these concepts.

1. Show students examples of conjunctions and interjections from literature.
The first step is to show the students examples of conjunctions and interjections from literature. Doing this allows the students to see what these grammatical concepts look like in good writing done by professional authors. Showing students examples of conjunctions and interjections from literature allows for discussion of why writers use them and what makes them important to good writing. This was the case in Ms. Fernandez's class; she showed her students examples of these grammatical concepts in a book the class had previously read. When doing this with your students, I recommend doing something similar to what Ms. Fernandez did: pick a book that your class has already read or is currently reading and show students examples of conjunctions and interjections from that book. Doing so will make the examples especially relevant and increase students' engagement in the lesson.

2. Remove the conjunctions and interjections and discuss the changed sentences.
I recommend removing the conjunctions and interjections from the published examples and discussing the changed sentences with students. This clearly demonstrates the importance of conjunctions and interjections to effective writing. When Ms. Fernandez removed the coordinating conjunction *and* from "Ben tripped over the curb, and Mary Lou gave me a peculiar look" (Creech, 1994, p. 136) to form "Ben tripped over the curb. Mary Lou gave me a peculiar look," the class could see the difference *and* made in this piece of writing. Without *and*, one sentence turned into two choppy ones.

I recently worked with a group of fifth graders who were reading Kathryn Lasky's book *Chasing Orion*. I knew that these students knew what conjunctions and interjections were, but I wanted them to understand why they are important to good writing. I began the activity by showing the students a passage from the book that contains an interjection: "'Look!'" I complained. "'All I did was ask an honest question'" (Lasky, 2010, p. 112).

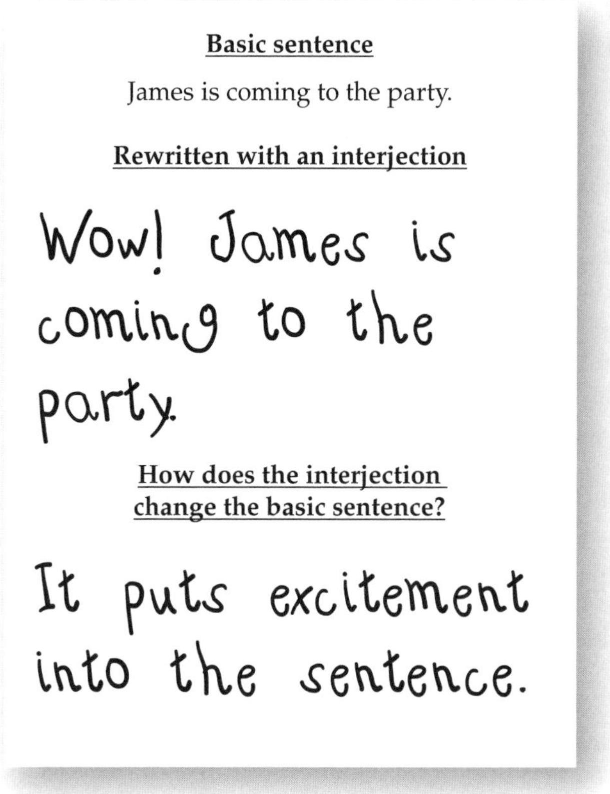

Figure 13.3 Student Work on Interjections

Basic sentence

James is coming to the party.

Rewritten with an interjection

Wow! James is coming to the party.

How does the interjection change the basic sentence?

It puts excitement into the sentence.

I talked with them about *look*'s being an interjection that expresses emotion, but until I rewrote the sentence without the conjunction and showed it to them, the students didn't really understand the difference. I brought over a nearby easel pad, wrote, "All I did was ask an honest question" and asked the students if they thought the tone in that sentence was different from the original text. After examining this example, one student remarked, "That one's really different. Without *look*, it doesn't sound the same, like it's not as strong." This analysis showed me that this student was beginning to understand that interjections are tools writers use to express emotion and say things strongly in their work.

3. Have students add conjunctions and interjections to basic sentences and reflect on the differences.

After students have analyzed altered versions of published sentences, I recommend giving them some basic sentences without conjunctions and interjections, asking them to add conjunctions and interjections to these sentences, and then helping them reflect on the differences. When I do this, I provide students with a sentence and ask them to add an interjection to it. After this, I give them two short sentences and ask them to link them using a conjunction. In each instance, I ask the students to reflect on how the new

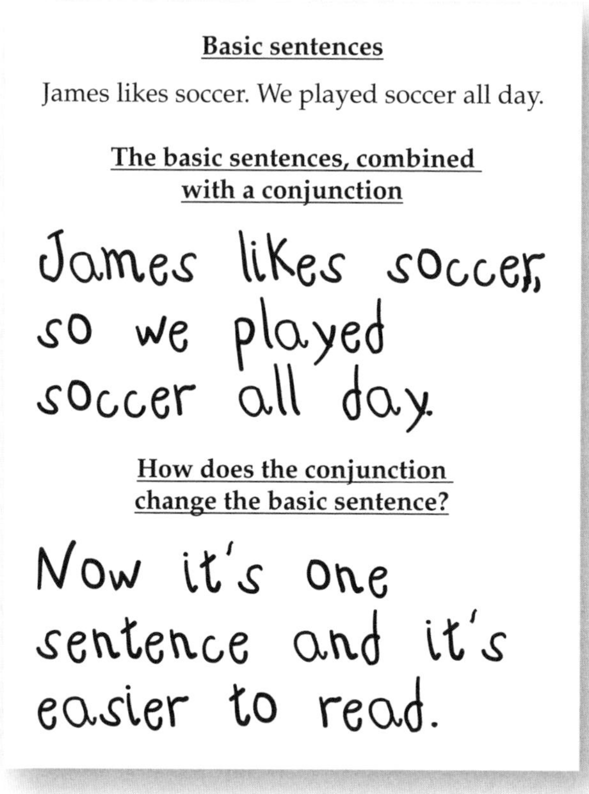

Figure 13.4 Student Work on Conjunctions

Basic sentences

James likes soccer. We played soccer all day.

The basic sentences, combined with a conjunction

James likes soccer, so we played soccer all day.

How does the conjunction change the basic sentence?

Now it's one sentence and it's easier to read.

sentence differs from the original text. This is a useful activity because the students can see the impact of the grammatical concepts *they* added.

Figure 13.3 (page 140) is an example of student work that focuses on the importance of interjections. This student, a young man named Thomas, added the interjection "Wow!" to the original sentence, "James is coming to the party" and noted that the interjection "puts excitement into the sentence."

Figure 13.4 (above) contains more of Thomas's work. In this situation, he focused on the uses of conjunctions, employing the conjunction *so* to link two choppy sentences. Note his response to how the conjunction changes the basic sentences: "Now it's one sentence, and it's easier to read."

When I talked with Thomas after he completed these activities, he noted that "adding these things really does a lot" for the quality of writing. Adding conjunctions and interjections to basic sentences helps students see how these grammatical concepts can improve a piece of writing.

The supplemental downloads (see page iv) contain templates from the activities that Thomas completed. One template contains the sentence to which Thomas added an interjection, and one template contains the short, choppy sentences that he linked with the word *so*. I suggest asking your students to complete these activities and then compare their work with partners' works, highlighting the different conjunctions and interjections each chose to use.

4. Ask students to look for places to add conjunctions and interjections to their writing.

The final step is to ask students to look for places to add conjunctions and interjections to their writing. This is an important step because it asks students to apply these concepts to their own work, which is the most authentic way to gauge students' understanding of grammatical concepts. To engage students, I recommend meeting with them individually to discuss the ways they have used conjunctions and interjections in their pieces, and situations in which they might include even more of these grammatical concepts. Because conjunctions and interjections have specific purposes, teachers don't want to force students to use those tools in situations where they're not needed. If there aren't any situations where students should add these grammatical concepts to their works, encourage them to keep the uses of conjunctions and interjections in mind as they continue to write.

Final Thoughts on Conjunctions and Interjections

The following information summarizes major points from this chapter, including what this grammatical concept is, why it's important for good writing, and how one might teach it for maximum effectiveness.

◆ Conjunctions and interjections are included in Common Core Language Standard 5.1.
◆ Conjunctions link statements together and can combine shorter sentences to form longer ones.
◆ There are three types of conjunctions: coordinating, correlative, and subordinating.
  • Coordinating conjunctions combine statements of equal importance. Some common examples are *for*, *and*, *nor*, *but*, *or*, *yet*, and *so*.
  • Correlative conjunctions are two-part structures that connect two related statements. Some common correlative conjunctions are *both-and*, *not only-but also*, *either-or*, and *neither-nor*.
  • Subordinating conjunctions link two statements when one is dependent on the other. Some common examples are *after*, *before*, *since*, and *when*.
  • Interjections are single words or short phrases used to express emotion, such as *wow*, *great*, and *no way*.
◆ Conjunctions are important to good writing because they allow authors to combine statements and avoid writing short, choppy sentences.

◆ Interjections are important to good writing because they allow authors to express emotion. They are especially important when writing dialogue and trying to show readers how a character is feeling.

◆ When teaching students about conjunctions and interjections, try these four things:

- Show students examples of conjunctions and interjections from literature.
- Remove the conjunctions and interjections and discuss the changed sentences.
- Have students add conjunctions and interjections to basic sentences and reflect on the differences.
- Ask students to look for places to add conjunctions and interjections to their writing.

14

Using Punctuation for Clarity and Effect

What Does "Use Punctuation for Clarity and Effect" Mean?

Common Core Language Standard 5.2 addresses the use of punctuation as part of a broader statement that students should "Demonstrate command of the conventions of standard English capitalization, punctuation, and spelling while writing" (Common Core Standards, 2010). Three specific requirements call for clear and purposeful punctuation use:

> "Use punctuation to separate items in a series."
> "Use a comma to separate an introductory element from the rest of the sentence."
> "Use a comma to set off the words *yes* and *no* (e.g., *Yes, thank you*), to set off a tag question from the rest of the sentence, (e.g., *It's true, isn't it?*), and to indicate direct address (e.g., *Is that you, Steve?*)."

The punctuation use addressed in this standard calls for writers to use punctuation for clarity and effect; in other words, it asks writers to use punctuation to produce clearly written works that convey their intended meanings. Sometimes forgetting to include a comma can lead to an unclear piece that is difficult to read; at other times, leaving out a comma can lead to an entirely different meaning. We'll look at specific examples of these instances later in this chapter, but first, let's look more closely at key components of Standard 5.2.

Use Punctuation to Separate Items in a Series

Writers use commas to separate the items in a series of three or more elements, such as "At the zoo, I saw the chimpanzees, the lions, and the giraffes." Separating the names of the animals with commas clearly shows that they are separate entities. Writing "I saw the chimpanzees the lions and the giraffes" would lead to confusion among readers because the animal names are not separated by commas. Commas are not needed to separate two items in a series, as in "I saw the chimpanzees and the lions."

Use a Comma to Separate an Introductory Element

Writers also use commas to separate introductory elements of sentences. An introductory element, found at the beginning of a sentence, provides information that is not essential to the sentence. For example, an introductory element can that tell when or where the events of the sentence happened. In the sentence "Inside the barn, John visited with the horses," "Inside the barn" is the introductory element; it opens the sentence by providing additional information about where the events of the sentence took place. A related sentence that also begins with an introductory element is "After the guests left, Joe also visited with the horses." In this sentence, the introductory element tells *when* the events of the sentence took place. Regardless of what specific information the introduction provides, it is still separated from the rest of the sentence by a comma.

Additional Examples of Commas and Separation

Common Core Standard 5.2 also calls for students to use commas to separate other aspects of sentences. Specifically, the standard requires separating the words *yes* and *no* from the rest of a sentence (No, I'm not going to the show), separating a question from the rest of a sentence (I haven't see the movie, have you?), and indicating direct address (John, are you playing in today's game?). In each example, a comma distinguishes between the main part of a sentence and additional information. By using commas in these situations, writers can clearly differentiate between the main part of a sentence and additional information. Note that in each of the examples included in parentheses in this section, the sentences could still exist without the information separated by commas. However, this additional information can provide important details that readers and writers alike may find useful.

Why Using Punctuation for Clarity and Effect Is Important to Good Writing

During a recent workshop at an elementary school, I met Joanna, a fifth-grade teacher struggling with teaching punctuation. "It's hard for me to teach punctuation, especially commas," she explained. "I just feel like I'm reciting a bunch of rules to the students, but I don't know how much they're retaining."

I identified with Joanna's situation: teaching punctuation is a challenge, especially if presented as a series of out-of-context rules that students need to memorize. Instead, punctuation instruction is much more effective if punctuation is viewed as a tool that writers use to create clearly written works that convey their intended meanings. If used correctly, punctuation can help writers get their ideas across as effectively as possible; if used incorrectly, it can result in readers being confused or, worse, misinterpreting the text.

The title of Lynn Truss's (2006) book *Eats, Shoots and Leaves* is an example of the potential impact of comma use; the title comes from a joke about a panda that highlights the importance of the comma following *Eats*. If this comma is used, the phrase means that the panda eats its food, shoots, and leaves the premises. If the title were rewritten as *Eats Shoots and Leaves*, it would refer to a panda's eating bamboo shoots and their leaves or eating shoots and then leaving the area. This example relates to the Common Core Standard 5.2's call for students to "Use punctuation to separate items in a series." With the comma after *Eats*, the words in this title make up a series of actions; without it, they state what the panda eats.

Another example of purposeful comma use is found in the following sentence from Gary Paulsen's novel *Hatchet*: "When he saw Brian look at him, the pilot seemed to open up a bit and he smiled" (Paulsen, 1987, p.6). This sentence's structure aligns with Common Core Standard 5.2's call for students to "Use a comma to separate an introductory element from the rest of the sentence." The comma between *him* and *pilot* makes this sentence easier to read by separating the introductory element "When he saw Brian look up at him" from the remainder of the sentence, and by telling readers to pause at that point in the sentence. Without this comma, nothing would distinguish the introductory element from the main part of the sentence, and readers would not be told to pause at that point. If the sentence doesn't have the comma (When he saw Brian look up at him the pilot seemed to open up a bit and he smiled), nothing separates these sentence parts, and the sentence is much more difficult to read.

In the novel *Lost in Cyberspace*, Richard Peck used commas to

- ◆ set off the word *no* from the remainder of the sentence,
- ◆ indicate direct address, and to
- ◆ separate a question from the rest of a sentence.

Each of these examples of comma usage aligns with one of the expectations of Common Core Standard 5.2. Peck used a comma to separate the word *No* from the remainder of a sentence when creating dialogue in which a character says, "No, they aren't. I put up that sign" (Peck, 1995, p. 92). This comma indicates that the word *no* can be separated from the rest of the sentence and shows that it provides additional information.

In the following passage from *Lost in Cyberspace*, Peck used a comma to indicate direct address and another to separate a question from the remainder of the sentence: "Aaron, you don't even remember those digits you entered when Phoebe suddenly turned up. You were winging it, right?" (Peck, 1995, p. 111). The comma following *Aaron* indicates direct address; it shows that the speaker is specifically talking to Aaron. Similarly, the comma before *right* separates the question word *right* from the rest of the sentence. This comma divides the statement "You were winging it" from "right?," which confirms the speaker's understanding of the situation. Without these commas and the information that accompanies them, Peck would not have been able to include the statement of direct address and the closing question. This passage from *Lost in Cyberspace* is an example of how commas connect important additional information to the main text of sentences.

As these examples from *Eats, Shoots and Leaves*, *Hatchet*, and *Lost in Cyberspace* indicate, commas are useful tools that writers use to clearly distinguish between ideas in their sentences. Whether the commas are used to distinguish between items in a series or separate questions, statements of direct address, or the words *yes* and *no* from the rest of a sentence, they are key elements of effective writing. Next, let's look at Ms. Fernandez's fifth-grade class and see how she engages her students in thinking about the importance of purposeful comma use.

A Classroom Snapshot

Ms. Fernandez again cheerfully greets me at her classroom door, this time sharing two pieces of information: (1) The students are doing an author study on novelist Virginia Hamilton, which they're really enjoying, and (2) she plans to use selections from Hamilton's novel *Bluish* (which the class has just completed) in the day's lesson on comma use, which is aligned with Common Core Language Standard 5.2. "We've been working on using commas, specifically as they relate to these rules," she explains, pointing to a description of Common Core Language Standard 5.2 written on the chalkboard. "I'm going to use some excerpts from *Bluish* to show some examples of the comma rules we've been talking about."

I smile, continuing to be thrilled at the way Ms. Fernandez is connecting grammar instruction with excerpts from literature. "Using examples from those books is a great idea," I reply. "It will really show the students how comma rules are put into practice by a great author." I sit down as Ms. Fernandez calls her students to attention.

"OK, everyone, eyes on the screen," Ms. Fernandez states, calling her students to focus on the screen in the front of the room, on which a PowerPoint presentation is about to be projected. "We've been talking about three major comma rules this week. This first slide you'll see will list all three of the rules." Ms. Fernandez clicks her computer and a slide appears, which lists the following guidelines for comma usage:

1. Commas separate three or more items in a series.
2. Commas are used in direct address.
3. Commas separate introductory elements from the rest of a sentence.

"We've talked about these rules, and I've shown you some examples I made up," explains Ms. Fernandez, "but today we're going to look at some examples written by Virginia Hamilton."

"The same one from our author study?" an intrigued student blurts out.

"The same," responds Ms. Fernandez. "I'm going to show you some examples from *Bluish*. In these examples, we'll see Virginia Hamilton using these comma rules in her writing."

Students look intently at the PowerPoint, while Ms. Fernandez turns to the next slide, which reads, "Dreen, she's in school with you" (Hamilton, 1999, p. 46). "Remember this sentence from *Bluish*?" she asks. Some students say yeah and yes before Ms. Fernandez continues. "In this sentence, Dreen's dad is talking to her. Why, do you think, did Hamilton use a comma after *Dreen*?"

Student hands fly up from tables all around the room; Ms. Fernandez calls on a student toward the front of the room, who explains, "Well, *Dreen* is the girl's name, so this shows her dad is talking to her. You use a comma when you're talking to someone and say the person's name."

"Exactly," replies Ms. Fernandez. "When we talk to someone directly and use his or her name, it is called 'direct address.' We always use commas when we use direct address. I'm going to show you another sentence from *Bluish* that goes with one of the comma rules we've been talking about."

Ms. Fernandez advances the PowerPoint to the next slide, revealing a new sentence from *Bluish*: "Dreenie, Bluish, and Paula were quick to understand the process" (Hamilton, 1999, p. 56). Ms. Fernandez reads the text aloud and asks the class, "Why are these commas in the sentence? Why did Virginia Hamilton use them?" As she says this, she points to the commas following *Dreenie* and *Bluish*.

A male student at one of the center tables answers, "They separate things—the people's names."

"Well said," answers Ms. Fernandez. "How does this relate to our comma rules?"

Another student responds, "One of the rules is that commas separate three or more things in a series, and this sentence has three things in it."

"Excellent," responds Ms. Fernandez. "The commas between these names separate three items in a series. The items are Dreenie, Bluish, and Paula. I'm going to show you one more sentence from *Bluish* that goes with another of the comma rules."

Ms. Fernandez changes to a new PowerPoint slide, which shows the following sentence from *Bluish*: "After they'd made a general plan, they could choose the size of the poster board and where they could put it" (Hamilton, 1999, p. 57). Ms. Fernandez points to the comma between *plan* and *they* and asks the class, "How about this comma? Why did Virginia Hamilton use this one?"

She looks out at the students, who seem hesitant to raise their hands, and inquires, "Can you relate it to one of our comma rules?"

A female student seated toward the back of the room replies, "Is this the rule about the introductory thing?"

"Yes, the introductory element," answers Ms. Fernandez. "Writers use commas to separate introductory elements from the rest of the sentence. What is an introductory element?"

The same student responds, "Something that introduces what's in the sentence."

"That's right. It's something that introduces what's in the sentence," replies Ms. Fernandez. "Remember, also, that an introductory element gives some kind of extra detail. The introductory element here is 'After they'd made a general plan.' It gives readers detail about when the thing described in the sentence could happen."

"So the introductory element is like extra information?" asks a student.

"That's correct," says Ms. Fernandez, "and that extra information is separated from the rest of the sentence by a comma." Ms. Fernandez then tells the students that their next task will be to look through their independent reading books and try to locate as many examples of these comma rules as they can. "Like Virginia Hamilton," she explains, "other writers also use commas in these ways. Try to find some examples in your free-reading books, and write down what you notice in your journals."

When I followed up with Ms. Fernandez shortly after the lesson, she said the students had done a good job of identifying examples of the comma rules in their independent reading books: "They picked out a lot of examples. Talking about [examples from] *Bluish* and having them look for commas in their free-reading books definitely helped them grasp these comma rules."

Recommendations for Teaching Students to Use Punctuation for Clarity and Effect

In this section, I describe a step-by-step instructional process to use when teaching students to use punctuation for clarity and effect:

1. Show students examples of punctuation rules from literature.
2. Have students search literature for examples of punctuation rules.
3. Show students sentences whose meanings vary with different punctuation use.
4. Ask students to create their own examples of sentences that vary with different punctuation use.
5. Have students examine the punctuation use in their own work.

Because these instructional steps are intended to be an application of students' knowledge of punctuation rules, I recommend discussing the

punctuation rules described at the beginning of this chapter before beginning this process.

1. Show students examples of punctuation rules from literature.

I recommend using literature to find examples of the punctuation rules
addressed in Common Core Language Standard 5.2. I also suggest showing students sentences from texts with which they are familiar, as this can
maximize their engagement and help them connect the punctuation rules
to works that are meaningful to them. After you present each sentence, ask
the students why the commas in the sentence are used in the ways they
are. For example, after Ms. Fernandez showed her students the sentence
"After they'd made a general plan, they could choose the size of the poster
board and where they could put it" (Hamilton, 1999, p. 57), she asked them
why Virginia Hamilton had used the comma between *plan* and *they*. This
allowed the students to apply their knowledge of punctuation to a familiar
text and helped them understand how writers use punctuation to make
their works as clear as possible.

2. Have students search literature for examples of punctuation rules.

After students discuss examples from literature as a whole class, I recommend asking them to work individually or in small groups and look
through other high-interest and grade-level-appropriate texts for examples of the same punctuation rules. The punctuation rules discussed in
Common Core Standard 5.2 are widely used, so most children's and young
adult books can be used for this activity. If students have independent
reading books that they bring to school, ask them to open these up and
look for examples of the punctuation rules you've discussed as a class.

3. Show students sentences whose meanings vary with different punctuation use.

The next step is to show students sentences whose meanings are dependent on their punctuation. Like the *Eats, Shoots and Leaves* example, the
variations in these sentence meanings are often humorous and can clearly
show students the way punctuation can impact the meaning of a sentence.

Figures 14.1 and 14.2 (page 152) contain examples I've used to show
students ways punctuation can alter the meaning of a sentence. In each
example, I write the same sentence twice on a large piece of paper but
punctuate it differently. The punctuation use in these sentences aligns with
elements of Common Core Language Standard 5.2. The sentences in Figure 14.1 highlight the importance of using a comma in direct address; those
in Figure 14.2 address the use of commas to separate items in a series.

After I show these sentences to a class, I discuss with the students
how the meanings of each pair vary and how punctuation plays a role
in those variations. When discussing the sentences in Figure 14.2, a fifth
grader with whom I worked explained, "This shows why you need to use

Figure 14.1 Using a Comma in Direct Address

Sentence One:

Let's leave, Bob.

Sentence Two:

Let's leave Bob.

Figure 14.2 Using a Comma to Separate Items in a Series

Sentence One:

He likes cooking, trees, and books.

Sentence Two:

He likes cooking trees and books.

commas to separate things. If you don't, there can be sentences like this where someone might think the wrong thing."

4. Ask students to create their own examples of sentences that vary with different punctuation use.

Next, I recommend asking students to create their own examples of sentences that vary with different punctuation use. This is typically an enjoyable activity for students because they can create sentences with humorous alternative meanings. One such example is Thomas's work, depicted in Figures 14.3 and 14.4 (page 153), which highlights the importance of using a comma to indicate direct address. In Figure 14.3, which contains the text "Let's eat, Grandma," Grandma is invited to dinner. However, in Figure 14.4, which contains the text "Let's eat Grandma," Grandma *is* dinner.

Figure 14.3 Student Work on Commas in Direct Address (Part 1)

Figure 14.4 Student Work on Commas in Direct Address (Part 2)

When I asked Thomas to comment on the importance of comma use in this piece, he explained: "I didn't know commas were important like this. [Now] I know they can really change what a writer is saying."

5. Have students examine the punctuation use in their own work.
I recommend concluding by asking students to examine the punctuation use in their own writing. This allows students to gain familiarity with the punctuation rules addressed in Common Core Standard 5.2 while also improving their own written works. I recommend giving students a clear, focused editing checklist that addresses the punctuation rules you've discussed as a class. This will ensure the students know exactly what to look for when they edit their work. Figure 14.5 (below) contains an example of an editing checklist I've used with students that is based on the punctuation rules in Common Core Language Standard 5.2. A printable version of this checklist is available as a supplemental download (see page iv).

Figure 14.5 Common Core Standard 5.2: Punctuation Editing Checklist

Instructions: Place a check in column three when you edit your writing for each punctuation requirement. Use the examples to remind yourself what that rule looks like in writing.

Punctuation Requirement	Example	Check When You Edit for This Requirement
Use punctuation to separate items in a series.	I like reading, running, and cooking.	
Use a comma to separate an introductory element from the rest of the sentence.	Before the show, Henry felt nervous and excited.	
Use a comma to set off the words *yes* and *no* from the rest of the sentence.	No, I won't be there today.	
Use a comma to set off a tag question from the rest of the sentence.	You'll be there, won't you?	
Use a comma to indicate direct address.	Jim, I'll see you at school.	

Final Thoughts on Using Punctuation for Clarity and Effect

The following information summarizes major points from this chapter, including what this grammatical concept is, why it's important for good writing, and how one might teach it for maximum effectiveness.

- ◆ Using punctuation for clarity and effect is related to the punctuation rules addressed in Common Core Standard 5.2.
- ◆ Three specific requirements call for clear and purposeful punctuation use:
  - • "Use punctuation to separate items in a series."
  - • "Use a comma to separate an introductory element from the rest of the sentence."
  - • "Use a comma to set off the words *yes* and *no* (e.g., *Yes, thank you*), to set off a tag question from the rest of the sentence, (e.g., *It's true, isn't it?*), and to indicate direct address (e.g., *Is that you, Steve?*)" (Common Core Standards, 2010).
- ◆ Punctuation instruction is most effective if punctuation is viewed as a tool that writers use to create clearly written works that convey their intended meanings.
- ◆ When teaching students about using punctuation for clarity and effect, try these five things:
  - • Show students examples of punctuation rules from literature.
  - • Have students search literature for examples of punctuation rules.
  - • Show students sentences whose meanings vary with different punctuation use.
  - • Ask students to create their own examples of sentences that vary with different punctuation use.
  - • Have students examine the punctuation use in their own work.

15

Dialects and Language Variations

What Are Dialects and Language Variations?

Common Core Language Standard 5.3 addresses the study of dialects and language variations. As part of a more general statement that students should "Use knowledge of language and its conventions when writing, speaking, reading, or listening," this standard specifically calls for students to "Compare and contrast the varieties of English (e.g., *dialects, registers*) used in stories, dramas, or poems" (Common Core Standards, 2010).

Dialect is defined as a "label to refer to any variety of language which is shared by a group of speakers" (Wolfram & Schilling-Estes, 1998, p. 250). Kolln and Funk (2009) explain that dialects often vary based on an individual's regional, ethnic, or social background. Three elements of language that often vary across dialects are terminology, sentence structure, and the plural form of *you*. Figure 15.1 (page 158) contains some examples of each of these linguistic elements that vary across dialects.

It's important to note that an individual might choose to use dialect in a particular situation. For example, someone might use the regional Southern term *y'all* in an informal setting with other speakers who share the same background, but choose not to use that term in a professional context. An individual who moves between informal and formal language is shifting between linguistic registers (Biber, 1995). The register in which one chooses to communicate can impact the level of regional, ethnic, or social dialect evident in one's language.

Common Core Standard 5.3 is particularly important because it asks students to do more than simply identify dialects in literature—it asks students to compare the dialects, registers, and language variations they find

Figure 15.1 Linguistic Elements That Vary Across Dialects

Linguistic Element	Example	Dialect Used in Example
Terminology	*Pop*: a term for a soft drink	*Pop* used this way is most commonly associated with the dialect of the Midwestern United States (Hall, 2002).
Sentence structure	Variations in expressing possession: "We are going to dad house."	Expressing possession without an apostrophe and an *s* is a feature of African American English (Wheeler & Swords, 2006).
Plural forms of *you* used	y'all, y'uns	Y'all is associated with southern dialects; y'uns is associated with midwestern and Appalachian dialects (Kolln & Funk, 2009).

in written works. In the next section, we'll consider why identifying and comparing these language variations is important to good writing.

Why Dialects and Language Variations Are Important to Good Writing

Dialects and language variations are tools that writers often use in dialogue to distinguish between characters and reveal aspects of their individual identities. When creating characters and establishing differences between them, writers often take into account how the characters speak. For example, when creating a character, writers may ask themselves the following questions about the character's language.

- ◆ Will this character speak in a dialect?
- ◆ Will this character speak in a formal or an informal register?
- ◆ What do these linguistic features show readers about this character?

The answers to these questions help an author establish a character's personality, style, and background. Paul Fleischman's novel *Seedfolks* is an example of an author using dialects and language variations to distinguish among characters. This novel, which describes a group of individuals who work together on a community garden in inner-city Cleveland, is told from a variety of perspectives. Each of the main characters has his or her own section, and Fleischman frequently varied the language in the sections to match the characters' personalities and backgrounds. For example, note the linguistic style Fleischman used when writing from the point of view of

Curtis, a young African American man: "Deltoids—awesome. Pecs—check 'em out. Quads—now playing on a body near you. Can't help being born with this body, or living three doors down from Kapp's gym. Can't stop people calling me Atlas or Ceps" (Fleischman, 1997, p. 51).

Now let's contrast that excerpt from Curtis's section with the following text, told from the point of view of a Korean woman named Sae Young: "We save all for children's college, so they can have easier life. But no children come. Very many years we hope, but still alone. Then my husband die. Heart attack" (Fleischman, 1997, p. 46). These examples show the purposeful language variation Paul Fleischman employed in *Seedfolks*, crafting Curtis's and Sae Young's language differently to show readers the differences in their backgrounds and personalities. If both of these characters spoke without language variations, readers would not get the sense of their identities that Fleischman's language choices supply.

Another example of an author using language variations to distinguish between characters is found in Jerry Spinelli's novel *Crash*. One way Spinelli illustrates the differences between two of the novel's main characters (Crash Coogan, a middle-school football star, and Penn Webb, a studious young man who tries out for cheerleading, gets involved in social issues, and is, in many ways, Crash's opposite) is through the ways they communicate. For example, let's look at the salutations Penn and Crash use. Penn greets his peers using formal language, such as "Greetings, fellow students," (Spinelli, 1996, p. 87); Crash is more casual, saying "How ya doin'?" (Spinelli, 1996, p. 83). These differing linguistic styles are tools Spinelli used to highlight the differences between these characters; the language they use represents their identities.

These examples illustrate the importance of language variation to effective writing. Fleischman and Spinelli use variations in the ways characters speak to distinguish them and reveal specific moods, personalities, and/or backgrounds. In the next section, we'll look at ways Ms. Fernandez helps her fifth-grade students understand how writers use language variations to establish characters' identities.

A Classroom Snapshot

One afternoon, after conducting a professional development session at Ms. Fernandez's school, I met with her about her plans for addressing some of the fifth-grade Common Core Language Standards in her upcoming lessons. "There's still one of these [standards] I can't figure out," she stated, "this one about the varieties of English: dialects and registers. I really don't know how to teach that."

I was so excited that Ms. Fernandez had raised this topic that my eyes lit up. We spent the next half hour chatting about novels that her students would enjoy that provided great examples of dialects and different registers. I told her how much I liked Paul Fleishman's novel *Seedfolks* and that it can be a great way to show students how authors use language to distinguish characters. At the end of this conversation, we made the following plan: after Ms. Fernandez and her students discussed what dialects and registers are and how they're used, the class would work with the "Curtis" section of *Seedfolks*, a section of the novel in which dialect really reveals the speaker's personality.

Let's fast-forward a week. It's a Wednesday morning, and I enter Ms. Fernandez's classroom as she is about to read the "Curtis" section from Paul Fleischman's novel *Seedfolks* with her students. All the students have copies of the book, but Ms. Fernandez is intent on reading it aloud so the students can hear Curtis's language and get the full experience of it. "I'll read this section aloud. I want you to follow along and really pay attention to Curtis's word choices. After we read, we're going to talk about how Curtis used dialect."

The students nod, and then listen as Ms. Fernandez begins. They listen closely as she reads the story of Curtis—a young man who tries to show responsibility and win back his former girlfriend by growing tomatoes, which she loves. As she reads, Ms. Fernandez pauses periodically to identify examples of dialect and informal language, such as "My homies all laughed to see me out there" (Fleischman, 1997, p. 55).

When Ms. Fernandez finishes reading this section, she asks the students to find examples of dialect that especially stood out to them and underline them. The students eagerly do so, having enjoyed the selection so much. Ms. Fernandez moves around the room, noting students' progress and commenting on their selections. She leans over next to a student who underlined "I could have banged their heads together and shut 'em up, but I didn't" (Fleischman, 1997, p.55) and says, "That's an outstanding choice. It's a good example of dialect and informal language, and it shows a lot about Curtis."

"Yeah, I think so too," the student responds.

After Ms. Fernandez circulates some more and remarks on the lines students have identified, she returns to the front of the classroom and tells the students what they'll do next. "Now that you've picked out these examples of dialect," she explains, "we'll move to the next step: translating the examples of dialect you identified into formal language. Draw a line down the middle of a piece of paper. On the left side, write the line from the text. On the right, rewrite it in formal language. Go ahead and get started, and let me know if you have questions."

The students begin work, and a few student hands pop up around the room. After Ms. Fernandez answers these students' questions, she continues to move around the classroom, checking on how the others are progressing. Pleased with their progress, Ms. Fernandez asks if anyone would like to share his or her work with the class.

A student seated at one of the tables in the front of the room raises her hand and begins: "I chose [the line from the text that reads]: 'I was showing Lateesha that just cause I got muscles don't mean I'm some jungle beast.'

I made it formal by changing it to 'I showed Lateesha that just because I am strong doesn't mean I can't be a gentleman.'"

"Excellent," responds Ms. Fernandez. "Who else would like to go?"

The student who previously picked out the line "I could have banged their heads together and shut 'em up, but I didn't" raises his hand, and Ms. Fernandez quickly calls on him. The student shares the line he identified from the section and explains, "I changed it to, 'I could have silenced them with violence, but I decided not to.'"

"Wonderful work," replies Ms. Fernandez. "Really nice change."

Later that week, I spoke to Ms. Fernandez about this lesson, as well as one she conducted the next day in which she talked with the students about how Curtis's section would be different without dialect. Ms. Fernandez explained that she was very pleased with the students' work. "They told me how important the dialect is for creating Curtis's character," she explained. "One of [the students] said that if Curtis didn't use dialect, he wouldn't sound like him, just like some robot or something. I thought that was a great way to put it."

Recommendations for Teaching Students About Dialect and Language Variation

In this section, I describe a step-by-step instructional process to use when teaching students to use punctuation for clarity and effect:

1. Show students examples of dialect in literature.
2. Ask students to change pieces of literature so they no longer include dialect.
3. Discuss with students how the piece is different without dialect.
4. Have students create characters and think about the language those characters will use.

These steps are intended to give students an opportunity to apply their knowledge of how writers use dialects and other language variations in their work. Because of this, I recommend discussing the definition of the term *dialect* and reviewing some examples with the students before beginning this process. I suggest using the information in the first part of this chapter, including the examples in Figure 15.1, to introduce this concept to the students. In addition, it's a good idea to discuss any dialects and regional variations specific to your students' communities.

1. Show students examples of dialect in literature.
I recommend showing students examples of dialect in literature. Doing this allows students to see how writers use dialects and other language variations to distinguish characters and allow characters' personalities to become apparent. Once you've talked with the students about what dialects are and why they're important to good writing, explain that you're

going to show them a piece of writing that contains examples of dialect. I suggest reading the piece aloud while your students follow along so they can hear the dialect and get a strong sense of how it impacts the tone of the piece. Once you do this, ask students to identify some examples of dialect from the text. Then you can gauge the students' understandings by checking the dialect they identified.

For example, when I conducted this activity with a group of fifth graders, I noticed that a couple of them identified selections from the text that were not actually examples of dialect. This showed me that these students still did not completely understand what dialect was. I met with these students and conducted a mini-lesson in which I talked further about what dialect is and showed them additional examples of dialect in literature. After this conversation, the students had much stronger understandings of dialect and were able to identify examples in literature more easily.

Although *Seedfolks* is an excellent example of literature that includes dialect, many other texts could be used for this purpose. Wheeler and Swords (2006) list the following picture books as some examples of texts that contain language variations: Carolivia Herron's *Nappy Hair* (1998) and Patricia McKissack's *Flossie and the Fox* (1986) and *A Million Fish . . . More or Less* (1992). Because so many books contain dialects or various linguistic registers, teachers have many options from which to choose. My advice is to look at texts that will interest your students and are in their general reading levels. Once you've identified books that fit these characteristics, you can look for examples of dialect that you'd like to bring into your classes.

2. Ask students to change pieces of literature so they no longer include dialect.

Once students have identified examples of dialect in literature, I recommend asking them to change those examples so they no longer include dialect. Removing examples of dialect and informal language and replacing them with formal language helps students see how important dialect and other language variations can be. Recall the student in Ms. Fernandez's class who changed the line "I was showing Lateesha that just cause I got muscles don't mean I'm some jungle beast" (Fleischman, 1997, p. 55) from Curtis's section of *Seedfolks* to "I showed Lateesha that just because I am strong doesn't mean I can't be a gentleman." Examining both of these lines reveals a sense of the importance of dialect to this piece. In the original text, readers get a strong sense of Curtis's personality and mood through the language he uses. In the revised sentence, readers can't make these same inferences. The language in this situation is formal and generic (or, as Ms. Fernandez's student put it, "like some robot.")

3. Discuss with students how the piece is different without dialect.

After the students revise the original work so it no longer includes dialect and informal language, help them discuss the differences in the pieces.

I recommend using a graphic organizer, such as the one in Figure 15.2, to help facilitate this discussion. This graphic organizer asks the students to list the original text and the new text they create. In addition, it asks students to answer two analytical questions: (1) How do you think the piece would be different if the character used formal language? (2) Why, do you think, did the writer choose to have the character communicate in the way he or she did? These analytical questions require students to consider an author's choices and incorporate the idea of questioning the author (Beck, McKeown, Hamilton, & Kucan, 1997), in which students enhance their comprehension and higher-order thinking skills by asking questions about an author's choices.

The graphic organizer I recommend using is shown in Figure 15.2 (page 164). It is also available as a supplemental download (see page iv).

Once students have completed this graphic organizer, you can use their responses to spark a discussion of why writers choose to have their characters communicate using dialect. To do this, I recommend asking students to share their graphic organizers with partners or small-group members. After they've done this, I suggest asking the class, "Based on what you wrote in your graphic organizer and our work today, why, do you think, do writers use dialect?" This question helps students think about dialect as a writing tool that authors purposefully implement for specific reasons, such as helping readers understand characters' personalities, backgrounds, and interests.

4. Have students create characters and think about the language those characters will use.

The final step of this process is to ask students to write original stories in which they create characters and think about the kind of language those characters will use. This will allow the students to put all the knowledge they've gained about language variation and dialect into practice. In addition, it will help them further understand that language variation is an important tool writers can use to distinguish characters by revealing those characters' identities and personalities. As students brainstorm for these stories, I recommend asking them to consider who the main character will be, what kind of language the character will use, and what the character's language will reveal about her or him. Figure 15.3 (page 165) shows a graphic organizer that students can use to plan their characters' linguistic practices. A blank version of this graphic organizer is included as a free supplemental download (see page iv).

I strongly recommend modeling this activity for students so their expectations of the task are clear, especially because students may not have previously considered a character's language when writing.

Showing students models like this one can give them a guiding example, which can help them think about the kinds of language their characters will use and how that language will reflect the characters' personalities.

Figure 15.2 Dialect Analysis Graphic Organizer

Original Text	New Text You Created	How do you think the piece would be different if the character used formal language?	Why, do you think, did the writer choose to have the character communicate in the way he or she did?

Figure 15.3 Model of Linguistic Practices Graphic Organizer

Character	What kind of language will this character use?	What will the character's language reveal about her or him?
Josh is a ten-year-old boy who loves baseball.	Josh will speak mostly in informal language, such as "yeah" and "what's up?" He'll use a lot of baseball slang. For example, he'll say that his fastball can "blow by" a hitter and that a ball that was hit hard was "crushed."	Josh's informal language will show that he's an easygoing guy. His baseball slang will show his love for the sport and how much time he spends playing, watching, and reading about it.

Final Thoughts on Dialects and Language Variations

The following information summarizes major points from this chapter, including what this grammatical concept is, why it's important for good writing, and how one might teach it for maximum effectiveness.

- Dialects and language variations are addressed in Common Core Standard 5.3, which calls for students to "Compare and contrast the varieties of English (e.g., *dialects*, *registers*) used in stories, dramas, or poems" (Common Core Standards, 2010).
- Dialect is defined as a "label to refer to any variety of language which is shared by a group of speakers" (Wolfram & Schilling-Estes, 1998, p. 250) and often varies based on an individual's regional, ethnic, or social background (Kolln & Funk, 2009).
- Dialects and language variations are tools that writers often use in dialogue to distinguish characters and reveal aspects of their individual identities.
- When creating characters and establishing differences between them, writers often take into account how the characters speak.
- When teaching students about how writers use dialect and language variations, try these four things:
  - Show students examples of dialect in literature.
  - Ask students to change pieces of literature so they no longer include dialect.
  - Discuss with students how the piece is different without dialect.
  - Have students create characters and think about the language those characters will use.

16

Figurative Language

What Is Figurative Language?

Common Core Language Standard 5.5 addresses the study of figurative language. As part of a statement that declares students should "Demonstrate understanding of figurative language, word relationships, and nuances in word meanings," this standard calls for students to "Interpret figurative language, including similes and metaphors, in context" (Common Core Standards, 2010).

Figurative language can be thought of as language that is not meant to be taken literally and is used to make writing more descriptive and add extra emphasis to a statement. To illustrate this, let's look at a statement with and without figurative language.

> **Example of a sentence with figurative language:**
> When the last day of school finally ended, the students ran **like cheetahs** out of the building.
> **Example of a sentence without figurative language:**
> When the last day of school finally ended, the students ran out of the building.

The sentence with figurative language contains a simile, which compares two unlike things using the words *like* or *as* to compare the students to cheetahs. This comparison is not to be taken literally; the sentence does not mean to say that the students ran with the speed of cheetahs or that they ran on four legs, as cheetahs do. Instead, the simile illustrates that the students ran quickly when leaving the building. The sentence without

Figure 16.1 Simile, Metaphor, and Personification

Type of Figurative Language	Definition	Example
Simile	Comparison of two different things using the words *like* or *as*	He jumped on the football **like** a lion pouncing on its prey.
Metaphor	Comparison of two different things that states one thing is another	Her **jacket is a shield** against the cold and rain, allowing her to stay warm and dry. Note: This sentence could also be written as "Her **jacket, a shield** against the cold and rain, allowed her to stay warm and dry." Sometimes authors will phrase metaphors in this way. Either phrasing tells the reader that the jacket is a shield against the cold and rain.
Personification	Giving human qualities to a nonliving thing	The **cold air crept** into our house.

figurative language does not contain this additional level of description and emphasis.

Three especially common forms of figurative language are similes, metaphors, and personification. Similes and metaphors are specifically mentioned in Common Core Language Standard 5.5; personification is another form of figurative language that is frequently taught in concert with similes and metaphors. Figure 16.1 (page 168) provides additional information about similes, metaphors, and personification.

Why Figurative Language Is Important to Good Writing

Figurative language is an important tool writers use to add description and emphasis to their work, making it easier for readers to clearly visualize what's taking place. In addition, figurative language can add "voice" to a piece of writing, allowing an author's or a character's distinctive style and personality to come through. Barone, Mallette, and Xu (2005) explain that authors can evaluate the voice in their works by asking questions such as "Does my paper sound like me?" and "How do I want my reader to feel?" (Barone et al., 2005, p. 130). Figurative language, such as similes, metaphors, and personification, can help a piece "sound like" a particular author or character by incorporating language specific to that individual's personality while also helping readers envision the situation.

For example, a writer describing a football game could say, "The players jumped on the loose ball." However, that same writer could use figurative language to add more description of the situation and allow readers to visualize it as clearly as possible, as in the sentence, "The players jumped on the loose ball like a group of hungry lions going after the last piece of meat." Both sentences describe the actions of the football players, but the example with figurative language helps readers picture the way the players jumped on the ball by using a simile to compare the players' actions to those of hungry lions. There is a sense of urgency in the sentence with figurative language that the other sentence does not possess.

In his novel *Sun & Spoon*, Kevin Henkes used figurative language to help readers visualize important images. For example, he used a simile to describe natural objects found on the hills in a cemetery: "And then there were the natural things—branches, twigs, leaves, and flower petals; they dotted the soft hills like a pattern on fabric" (Henkes, 1997, p.113). In this sentence, the simile "like a pattern on fabric" helps the image come alive; it allows readers to compare the branches, twigs, leaves, and flower petals on the hills to a fabric pattern's markings. Henkes's skillful use of this simile helps readers "see" the image described in the text and compare it to another familiar object, creating an easy-to-visualize picture.

Another text in which figurative language helps readers clearly visualize significant details is Avi's novel *Perloo the Bold*. In the following passage, Avi used a simile to help readers visualize a nervous character's movements: "Nose quivering, glossy ears shaking like aspen leaves, Berwig hopped awkwardly to where Perloo and Lupacabra were standing" (Avi, 1998, p. 19). The simile "like aspen leaves" helps readers visualize the intensity with which Berwig's ears were shaking, highlighting the anxiety he feels.

Avi again used a simile in *Perloo the Bold* to clearly capture the details of an event. After describing a heavy snowfall, Avi explains, "The snow became jagged bits of ice that wiggled like frigid worms into every nook and crevice of their smocks" (Avi, 1998, p. 86). The simile "like frigid worms" is important to this sentence because of the mental image it can create for readers. Without this simile, readers would still learn of the wiggling jagged bits of ice; however, the comparison of these pieces of ice to frigid worms helps readers understand the way the bits of ice moved and visualize them doing so.

In her novel *Tuck Everlasting*, Natalie Babbitt used a metaphor in the sentence, "The sun was dropping fast now, a soft red sliding egg yolk, and already to the east there was a darkening to purple" (Babbit, 1975, p. 60). This sentence states that the setting sun was "a soft red sliding egg yolk," allowing readers to clearly envision its color and shape. Without this metaphor, readers would not benefit from such a clear, specific description of the visual aspects of this sunset.

These examples from *Sun & Spoon*, *Perloo the Bold*, and *Tuck Everlasting* illustrate that figurative language is an important tool that writers use when creating descriptive images that are easy for readers to visualize. Though the sentences from the novels included in this section would still make sense without the figurative language the authors chose to include, they certainly would not have the level of detailed description that helps make them such high-quality sentences. Readers would probably not be able to clearly envision the natural objects dotting the cemetery hills without Henkes's comparison of those items to a pattern on fabric. Similarly, it would be much harder to picture Berwig's nervousness or the specific way the jagged pieces of ice wiggled without Avi's similes, and readers would not be able to visualize the colorful sunset Babbitt intended them to imagine without her effective metaphor.

Students can apply figurative language to their own work in similar ways, using published texts as models and ultimately using this strategy to make their writing detailed and easy to envision. Next, we'll look at how Ms. Fernandez uses Sharon Creech's novel *Walk Two Moons* in an engaging lesson designed to help students understand the importance of figurative language.

A Classroom Snapshot

I enter Ms. Fernandez's classroom, hang up my coat, sit down in a chair near the back of the room, and wait excitely for the lesson on figurative language to begin. During the past week, I've communicated with Ms. Fernandez about this lesson, in which she and her students will discuss the figurative language addressed in Common Core Language Standard 5.5. "I want to show them some examples from *Walk Two Moons*," (a novel by Sharon Creech the class read earlier in the school year) she explained. "There's a lot of figurative language in [that book], so I thought that would be a good connection. Plus, it went well when we used [*Walk Two Moons*] to talk about conjunctions and interjections."

"That's fantastic," I responded. "This will really help your students understand why figurative language is important to good writing." Ms. Fernandez agreed and explained to me that, after spending a couple of days introducing figurative language to her students and making sure they understand the differences between simile, metaphor, and personification, she would show her students some examples of figurative language from *Walk Two Moons* and discuss with them the importance of these examples. For the lesson described here, the class's first time using *Walk Two Moons* to discuss figurative language, Ms. Fernandez decided to focus specifically on similes in the text (she and her students discussed metaphors and personification in *Walk Two Moons* in subsequent lessons).

Ms. Fernandez opens the lesson with a few PowerPoint slides review-ing the definition of figurative language and some examples of simile, met-aphor, and personification. "This is what we've been talking about in our last two classes," she explains, "but today we're going to take it in a differ-ent direction. Remember the book *Walk Two Moons*?" Students around the classroom nod. "We read it earlier in the year, and we talked about some examples from it recently when we worked on conjunctions and interjec-tions. Today, we're going to look at some similes in it."

Ms. Fernandez clicks to access the next PowerPoint slide, which con-tains the following text from *Walk Two Moons*: "Just over a year ago, my father plucked me up like a weed and took me and all our belongings . . . and stopped in front of a house in Euclid, Ohio" (Creech, 1994, p. 1). "Take a look at this sentence," she instructs her students. "Does anyone see any similes?"

"'Like a weed,'" a student replies.

"The simile is 'like a weed,'" echoes Ms. Fernandez. "Right on the first page of the novel, the author used a simile. How about that! How do you think this sentence would be different if it didn't have this simile?"

Ms. Fernandez calls on a boy in the back of the classroom, who states, "It wouldn't be as interesting."

"An excellent start," replies Ms. Fernandez. "What do you mean by interesting?"

"Well," he responds, "it's like the same basic stuff would be there, but it wouldn't be described in as interesting a way."

As the student finishes, another raises her hand and states, "The sim-ile makes it so you can picture the father picking her up like you pluck a weed."

"So, if we didn't have this simile, we couldn't picture what happened as clearly?"

The student replies in the affirmative, while others also nod yes.

"That's an outstanding point," continues Ms. Fernandez. "Sometimes figurative language, such as similes, can help us really picture what we read or really understand what's happening. I'm going to give each table a sentence from *Walk Two Moons* that contains a simile. I want you to find the simile and talk about why it is important to that sentence. Once each table group is done, someone from each table will read the example for the class and tell us why the simile in that sentence is important."

Ms. Fernandez walks around the room, giving each table a piece of paper containing a passage from *Walk Two Moons* that contains a simile:

- ◆ "The houses were all jammed together like a row of birdhouses" (p. 2).
- ◆ ". . . when my grandparents got in a car, trouble just naturally followed them like a filly trailing behind a mare" (p. 5).
- ◆ "Sometimes I am as ornery and stubborn as an old donkey" (p. 6).

- ◆ "There were Megan and Christy, who jumped up and down like parched peas. . . . " (p. 12).
- ◆ "My grandparents can get into trouble as easily as a fly can land on a watermelon" (p. 26).

The students work in groups, identifying the similes in the passages and then discussing why those similes are important to the sentence. After they've taken several minutes to do this, Ms. Fernandez asks for a group to read its passage to the class, identify the simile, and describe why the simile is important to the text. The first group to volunteer stands up and shares its insights. One of the group members begins by saying that the students worked with the text that reads ". . . when my grandparents got in a car, trouble just naturally followed them like a filly trailing behind a mare." The student continues to explain, "The simile is 'like a filly trailing behind a mare.'"

"And why is that simile important to the sentence?" asks Ms. Fernandez.

"The simile's important," replies another student in the group, "because it gives a comparison. It compares trouble following the grandparents with a filly following a mare."

"Yeah," interjects another student in the group. "[This comparison] shows how trouble follows the grandparents. It shows that it's natural for trouble to follow them like it's natural for a filly to follow a mare."

After Ms. Fernandez applauds this group's response, the other four groups share similarly strong analyses of the similes in their excerpts. When the last group finishes, Ms. Fernandez concludes the language arts period by praising the students: "Excellent work, everyone, on describing how the similes in these examples are important."

Recommendations for Teaching Students About Figurative Language

In this section, I describe a step-by-step instructional process to use when teaching students about figurative language:

1. Show students passages from literature that contain figurative language, and discuss the importance of the figurative language in those passages.
2. Have students create written works that contain figurative language.
3. Ask students to remove the figurative language from their work and then consider how that version of the piece is different from the original.
4. Ask students to reflect on why figurative language is important to good writing.

Because these steps are intended to be an application of students' knowledge of figurative language, I recommend discussing the definitions and examples of figurative language described at the beginning of this chapter before beginning this process.

1. Show students passages from literature that contain figurative language and discuss the importance of the figurative language in those passages.

I recommend showing students examples from literature that contain figurative language and talking with them about how that language is important to the piece. This provides a useful application of the students' knowledge of figurative language. I like to tell students, "Now that you've learned what figurative language is, you're ready to see how authors use it." Once I present students with an example of a published work that contains some form of figurative language, I talk with them, as Ms. Fernandez did, about what kind of figurative language is contained in the text and how it enhances the piece. One particularly effective element of Ms. Fernandez's lesson was the way she led a whole-class discussion on this topic and then asked the students to do the same kind of analysis in their small groups. This showed the students how to identify and discuss figurative language before asking them to do it on their own. I recommend doing a similar activity with your students—analyze the figurative language in a text as a whole class and follow that up by asking students to conduct a similar analytic activity in small groups.

2. Have students create written works that contain figurative language.

Once students have analyzed the figurative language in published works and commented on how the figurative language impacts those pieces, it's time to ask them to create their own pieces of writing that contain figurative language. I tell students that they can write in any genre as long as they use a certain number of examples of figurative language. For example, when recently working with a fifth-grade class, I asked the students to create written work with at least one simile, one metaphor, and one example of personification. Figure 16.2 (page 174) depicts one fifth-grader's work on this activity; Jessica's Halloween poem contains one example of each of these forms of figurative language.

In her poem, Jessica used the simile "like cars in rush hour traffic" to describe the children crowding the streets and the metaphor "the jack o' lanterns are lighthouses" to depict how they guide the way in the night. In addition, she incorporates personification by saying "The pirate costume in my closet is calling my name." These examples of figurative language enhance the level of description in the piece. After students create these works, I invite them to share them with their peers by reading them aloud and pointing out the figurative language used in each piece. This

Figure 16.2 Student Work With Figurative Language

Halloween Poem With Figurative Language

It is a cold October night
The coldest of the year so far
But I still feel a warmth that
    excites me
Children crowd the streets like cars
    in rush hour traffic
And the jack o'lanterns are
    lighthouses guiding the way

This has always been my favorite
    holiday
I hope I never grow too old for it

Bring on the candy the costumes,
    the trick or treaters
The pirate costume in my closet is
    calling my name
Halloween is finally here

can facilitate discussions of how the figurative language in each piece adds description that would not otherwise be there.

3. Ask students to remove the figurative language from their work and then consider how that version of the piece is different from the original.

After students have created and shared these works, I recommend asking them to revise the pieces so they no longer contain figurative language. Though this might sound counterintuitive in a lesson on figurative language, I've found this process really shows students the differences in quality between pieces that contain figurative language and those that don't. By initially creating works that contain figurative language, students get experience describing elements of their pieces in detailed and engaging ways. When they're forced to eliminate that language, they can see that their descriptions no longer contain the detail and distinctiveness that figurative language provides.

Figure 16.3 (page 175) shows the revised version of Jessica's Halloween Poem depicted in Figure 16.2. For the new version, Jessica removed the figurative language. The simile that compares the children to cars in rush hour traffic is gone, as is the metaphor that states, "the jack o' lanterns are

**Halloween Poem Without
Figurative Language**

It is a cold October night
The coldest of the year so far
But I still feel a warmth that
    excites me
Children crowd the streets
And the jack o'lanterns guide the
    way

This has always been my favorite
    holiday
I hope I never grow too old for it

Bring on the candy the costumes,
    the trick or treaters
I can't wait to wear the pirate
    costume in my closet
Halloween is finally here

Figure 16.3 Student's Poem Without Figurative Language

lighthouses." In addition, the pirate costume is no longer personified; the text now reads, "I can't wait to wear the pirate costume in my closet."

When I asked Jessica to compare the two pieces, she explained, "I like the one with figurative language a whole lot better. The simile, metaphor, and personification make that one much more descriptive. I think the second one is more dull."

4. Ask students to reflect on why figurative language is important to good writing.

As a final step, I recommend asking the students to consider why figurative language is important to good writing. To do this, I recommend reviewing with students the published texts you discussed together and then asking them to conduct a think-pair-share on the following question: "Based on this example and the pieces you created, why is figurative language important to good writing?" When recently conducting this activity with a fifth-grade class, I was impressed with the quality of the students' responses. One student explained that the figurative language helped writers use their own style; another said that figurative language makes writing easier to picture. These comments showed me that the students had developed a strong awareness of why writers use figurative language and suggested that they were thinking metacognitively about the topic.

Final Thoughts on Figurative Language

The following information summarizes major points from this chapter, including what this grammatical concept is, why it's important for good writing, and how one might teach it for maximum effectiveness.

- ♦ Figurative language is addressed in Common Core Language Standard 5.5, which calls for students to "Interpret figurative language, including similes and metaphors, in context" (Common Core Standards, 2010).
- ♦ Figurative language can be defined as language that is not meant to be taken literally. It is an important tool writers use to add description and emphasis to their works, making it easier for readers to clearly visualize what's taking place.
- ♦ Figurative language can also add "voice" to a piece of writing, allowing for an author or a character's distinctive style and personality to come through.
- ♦ Three especially common forms of figurative language are similes, metaphors, and personification.
  - Similes compare two different things using the words *like* or *as*.
  - Metaphors compare two different things by stating that one thing is another.
  - Personification is giving human qualities to a nonliving thing.
- ♦ When teaching figurative language, remember:
  - Show students passages from literature that contain figurative language and discuss the importance of the figurative language in those passages.
  - Have students create written works that contain figurative language.
  - Ask students to remove the figurative language from their work and then consider how that version of the piece is different from the original.
  - Ask students to reflect on why figurative language is important to good writing.

Section **4**

Putting It Together

17

Assessing Students' Knowledge

How Can Teachers Best Assess Students' Knowledge of the Grammar Toolkit?

A significant part of grammar instruction is coming up with assessments that provide accurate and meaningful measures of student learning. Because it's important to connect assessment and instructional practices (Bratcher & Ryan, 2004), the best grammar assessments are those that are tied to the kinds of instruction provided to students. In this chapter, I discuss two kinds of assessment methods that are related to the instructional practices described in this book. The first involves providing students with examples from literature that contain particular grammatical concepts and asking students how those grammatical concepts enhance the writing. The second involves asking students to create works that contain specific grammatical concepts and then having them explain the importance of those grammatical concepts to the texts they created. In this chapter, I discuss these assessment practices and explain how each can be used as both summative and formative assessments.

These assessment methods were designed to measure students' understandings of the hows and whys of grammar, specifically, how authors use grammatical concepts and why these concepts can enhance writing. The assessments move past the basic drills and textbook exercises that Robb (2001), Weaver (1998), and others caution against, instead asking students to utilize higher-order thinking skills and metacognitive thinking while completing grammar assessments. Let's look at each of these methods in more detail.

Assessment Method 1: Literary Analysis

In this assessment method, students conduct a type of literary analysis by examining examples from literature that contain particular grammatical concepts and describing how those concepts enhanced the writing. I have found this to be a useful method because it requires students to read a work of literature critically with the author's use of grammatical concepts in mind. These kinds of critical readings are related to the instructional practices described in this book that involve showing students examples of a particular grammatical concept in literature and discussing how the author used that concept.

Let's discuss exactly what such an exercise would look like. In an assessment about prepositional phrases, I would provide students with an example from literature that contains a prepositional phrase, as well as an adapted version of that sentence that *does not* contain the prepositional phrase. I'd ask the students to read the sentences and explain how the prepositional phrase enhances the piece. When creating these exercises, you can certainly use any of the literary examples from this book, provided those examples are on your students' reading levels. Below is an example of a question from an assessment on prepositional phrases. This question used a sentence from Jerry Spinelli's novel *Maniac Magee*.

Below is an excerpt from *Maniac Magee* with a prepositional phrase underlined.
"And sometimes Maniac just sat <u>at the front window</u>. . . . " (Spinelli, 1990, p. 56)

Below is the same excerpt from *Maniac Magee* without the prepositional phrase.
"And sometimes Maniac just sat. . . . "

In the space below, describe how the prepositional phrase in the sentence improves the piece. Then explain why you believe the author used it.

These exercises ask students to think metacognitively about how the phrase enhances the work. Though prepositional phrases add details to a text, other grammatical concepts, such as subject-verb agreement and pronoun reference, are used to ensure that a piece of writing is clear and that readers and writer can envision the same thing. When assessing students on these kinds of concepts, I provide them with a sentence from a published work as well as an incorrect version that does not use the focal concept properly.

I ask the students to compare the passages by explaining why the example with the correctly used grammatical concept is clearer than the incorrect example. Following is a sample question from an assessment on pronoun reference. This example uses a passage from Mary Pope Osborne's novel *Sunset of the Sabertooth*, previously discussed in chapter 1 of this book.

Below is a passage from *Sunset of the Sabertooth* that contains correct pronoun reference.
"Annie held the rope with both hands. She pushed her feet against the side of the pit. **She** rose into the air with the rope" (Osborne, 1996, p. 45).

Below is the same example from *Sunset of the Sabertooth* with one change: it no longer contains correct pronoun reference.
"Annie held the rope with both hands. She pushed her feet against the side of the pit. **They** rose into the air with the rope."

In the space below, compare the two sentences by explaining why the sentence with correct pronoun reference is clearer than the one with incorrect pronoun reference. Then answer this question: Based on these sentences, why is it important that writers use correct pronoun reference?

This exercise was designed to ask students to think metacognitively about why a particular grammatical concept—in this case, pronoun reference—is important to good writing. Now, let's look at the second assessment method in this approach: student-created texts and analysis.

Assessment Method 2: Student-Created Texts

In this assessment method, students create their own works that contain specific grammatical concepts and then explain the importance of those grammatical concepts to the pieces they created. This form of assessment is similar to assessment method 1 in some ways and different in others. The two methods are similar because they both ask students to critically analyze how a particular grammatical concept can improve a piece of writing. They are different because the first assessment method involves students' analyzing a piece of literature written by a published author, and the second asks the students to create their own works and discuss how the grammatical concept impacted those works. I have found that this assessment method makes the material even more relevant for students because they are reflecting on how specific grammatical concepts impact their own work.

Let's look at how some of these kinds of examples could appear on an assessment. If I were giving students a test on prepositional phrases, I would provide them with the following instructions.

> **In the space below, create a piece of writing that contains at least three prepositional phrases. Underline each prepositional phrase. The piece can be in any genre and can describe fictional or nonfictional events.**
>
>
>
> **In the space below, describe how the prepositional phrases contribute to your piece. What kinds of information would your readers not have if you didn't use prepositional phrases? Be specific.**

Now let's look at an assessment issue that focuses on a different kind of grammatical concept, such as pronoun reference, that deals more with ensuring clarity than with adding detail. In an assessment on pronoun reference, I would provide students with the following instructions.

> **In the space below, create a piece of writing that contains correct pronoun reference. Make sure the pronouns and antecedents in your piece agree. Underline at least three pronouns in your piece. The piece can be in any genre and can describe fictional or nonfictional events.**

> **In the space below, describe how the clear pronoun reference in your piece contributes to the meaning of it. How would your piece be confusing if you didn't use correct pronoun reference? Be specific.**

The assessment examples on prepositional phrases and those on pronoun reference both ask students to do the following:

◆ Create a piece of writing that uses a specific grammatical concept.
◆ Identify examples of that concept.
◆ Explain why the use of that grammatical concept contributes to the quality of the piece.

This assessment method can be applied to any grammatical concept; these are just two particular examples. Next, let's explore how one might grade these assessment questions.

Grading the Assessment Examples

I recommend using a rubric that allows students to earn up to 10 points for each question—5 for the accuracy of the information in their responses and 5 for the quality of the analysis. If the assessment contains two problems (one on literary analysis and one on student-created text), then students can earn up to 20 points. Figure 17.1 (page 184) shows a rubric I've used to assess student responses to these exercises; it contains the areas of evaluation, evaluation questions I use to assess the students' responses, the possible points for each section, and places to record the students' scores and comment on their work.

This is the rubric I use to evaluate responses on the grammatical concept test. Each response can earn up to 10 total points—5 for the accuracy of the information and 5 for the quality of the analysis. The questions below describe what I'm looking for when I grade the responses.

These two rubric criteria combine to evaluate two things: (1) the accuracy of the information in students' responses, and (2) the quality of the analysis in those responses. I give the students a copy of the rubric before the test so they can see how I'll evaluate their work.

Summative and Formative Assessments

The kinds of assessment problems and examples described in this chapter can be used as summative assessments (those used at the end of a unit of study) as well as formative assessments (in-process assessments used

Figure 17.1 Rubric for Grammatical Concept Assessment

Area of Evaluation	Evaluation Questions	Possible Points	Your Score
Accuracy of information	Is the information in the response correct? Is it clear from the response that the author has an excellent understanding of the grammatical concept?	5	
Quality of analysis	Are all components of the response described in detail? Does the author show an excellent understanding of how writers use the grammatical concept? Is it clear that the author has thought about how this grammatical concept can improve a piece of writing?	5	
Total score:			
Comments:			

during a unit to measure how well students are learning the material and what adjustments a teacher might make to help the students better understand the content). This section discusses how to use these assessment examples for both summative and formative purposes.

Summative Assessments

I recommend giving students focused tests on individual grammatical concepts rather than giving them one large test on many concepts together. For example, I recommend giving fourth graders separate assessments on prepositional phrases, relative pronouns and adverbs, modal auxiliaries, and other key concepts discussed in the Common Core Standards instead of giving them a cumulative exam that covers all of these topics at one time. I believe that conducting separate assessments allows students to demonstrate their knowledge of each grammatical concept in depth without overwhelming them. When I create a summative assessments, I include two elements—one literary analysis problem and one student-created text and analysis. I then grade each response using the rubric depicted in Figure 17.1.

Formative Assessments

The assessment examples described in this chapter can also make excellent tools for formative assessments, which students complete during a unit to provide feedback and insight into how much they've learned and what they still need to know. When I use one of these problems as a formative assessment, I ask students to respond to it at the end of a language arts class as an "exit question." Then, I read the students' answers and gauge their progress. I prefer not to grade students on these assessments but rather to respond with comments that highlight what they've done well and call attention to elements of the response that are incorrect or that could benefit from further development and clarification. This helps the students use their responses and my feedback to prepare for the summative assessments, where they will see these kinds of problems again. In addition, I use formative assessments to guide my instruction—if it's clear from the assessments that my students are having a hard time with a grammatical concept, I'll return to the concept and work to clarify students' understanding. Based on the number of students who demonstrate difficulty with a concept, I either instruct the whole class on the topic or identify a group of students that need extra support and conduct a mini-lesson with them.

Final Thoughts on Assessing Students' Knowledge

The following information summarizes key ideas about assessing students' knowledge of important grammatical concepts:

- ◆ I recommend assessing students' knowledge of grammatical concepts in two different ways: (1) literary analysis, and (2) student-created texts.
  - In literary analysis problems, students examine examples from literature that contain particular grammatical concepts and describe how those concepts enhanced the writing.
  - In student-created texts and the corresponding analysis, students create their own works that contain specific grammatical concepts and then explain the importance of those grammatical concepts to the writing.
- ◆ The assessment examples described in this chapter can be used as both summative and formative assessments.
  - I recommend giving students summative assessments on specific grammatical concepts and including one literary analysis problem and one student-created text and analysis on each test.
  - I recommend using these kinds of problems as formative assessments by asking students to respond to them informally as end of class "exit questions" and using the students' responses to assess their understandings and inform future instruction.

Conclusion
Final Thoughts and Tips for Classroom Practice

How Do I Put the Ideas in This Book Into Action?

At a recent conference, I spoke to a teacher named Mary about grammar instruction. Mary, who was in her 21st year as an elementary-school teacher, shared her thoughts on the challenges of grammar instruction. "I think it's so hard to teach students grammar in a way that helps them apply what they learn to their writing. I've been struggling with this for a while." She continued, "Grammar can be easy to teach, but I think it's hard to teach well." Mary and I talked about the ideas described in this book and some ways to put these ideas into action. I told her, "One of the things I like most about this approach is it's really fun to put into action. Once students understand the concepts, you're really talking with them about literature and writing. Grammar becomes a part of that conversation."

In this chapter, we'll look at some tips for putting the ideas in this book into practice in your classroom. Though each chapter in this book provides specific recommendations for teaching a grammatical concept, the recommendations below provide a general framework for grammar instruction that connects grammatical concepts to the characteristics of effective writing and shows students that these concepts are tools that writers use to enhance their work.

Tips for Classroom Practice
- Discuss the nuts and bolts of a specific grammatical concept.
- Show students examples from literature of that concept.
- Discuss why the grammatical concept is important to the piece of literature.
- Have students use the concept in their own writing.
- Ask students to reflect on the concept's uses.

In the following sections, I describe each tip in additional detail, providing insight into how to incorporate them into the classroom.

Discuss the Nuts and Bolts of a Grammatical Concept
Before talking with students about why a particular grammatical concept is important to good writing, it's important to discuss the fundamentals, or the nuts and bolts, of that concept. Each chapter in this book begins with

important fundamental information about its focal concept. I recommend using the examples and figures in those sections to introduce grammatical concepts to students and discuss their defining characteristics with them. Once students are comfortable with this information, they can move forward to thinking analytically and metacognitively about grammar.

Show Students Examples From Literature of That Concept

The next step in this process is to show students examples from literature of the grammatical concept you're discussing. It's best to select examples from texts that interest your students and are at their general reading level. Each chapter in this book contains examples from children's or young adult literature of particular grammatical concepts. These can be great examples to use, but you should also feel free to select different ones based on the interests and needs of your students. Regardless of which literary examples you use, this is an excellent practice because it shows students that grammatical concepts don't just exist in isolated grammar exercises—instead, they are found in literature and are tools published writers use.

Discuss Why the Grammatical Concept Is Important to the Piece of Literature

This instructional practice is a logical follow-up to the previous one; after you show students examples from literature of a particular grammatical concept, talk with them about why that grammatical concept is important to the pieces of literature. The specific conversation you'll have about this topic will vary based on the grammatical concept. A discussion about why a published writer used figurative language would be different from one that focuses on subject-verb agreement, but each conversation should be based on the same "big idea": how does the use of this grammatical concept enhance this piece of literature? Class discussions and corresponding activities that address this question can help students understand that grammatical concepts are used purposefully in writing and can enhance written works in specific ways.

Have Students Use the Concept in Their Own Writing

After students understand why a specific grammatical concept enhances a published text, the next step is to ask them to use that concept in their own writing. If students are already working on a particular piece of writing, you can ask them to use the grammatical concept you're studying. For example, if you're discussing relative clauses with your students, ask them to incorporate some relative clauses in the pieces they're working on. If students aren't currently working on pieces, you can ask them to create short pieces that incorporate the grammatical concept on which you're focusing. Asking students to apply specific grammatical concepts to their writing can help them see that these concepts are useful tools that can enhance the quality of that writing.

Ask Students to Reflect on the Concept's Uses

Finally, I recommend asking students to reflect on the uses of the grammatical concept on which you are focusing. To engage students in this kind of reflection, I first ask them to think about how they used the grammatical concept in their own writing. To facilitate this, I ask the students to find an example of the focal concept in their writing and explain what it does to enhance the piece. After students share their responses with the class, I ask them, usually in a think-pair-share format, to reflect on why this concept is an important tool for effective writing. I always love hearing what the students share; their insights into how grammatical concepts can enhance writing frequently show that they are thinking metacognitively about grammar and are poised to apply these concepts to their future work.

Final Thoughts: The Journey of Innovative Grammar Instruction

The ideas discussed in this book are rooted in the belief that grammatical concepts are important tools that writers use to enhance the quality of their work. As students work on mastering the Common Core Language Standards and the grammatical concepts described in them, it's important to emphasize the essential role that grammar plays in creating clear, descriptive writing. I hope that the ideas, texts, and examples discussed in this book help you and your students have meaningful conversations about grammar's role in works of literature written by published authors and the writing that your students create. Grammar instruction that is linked with literature and writing provides a pedagogically sound and research-based alternative to the conventional work sheets and out-of-context grammar exercises that Weaver (1998) and other grammar experts tell teachers to avoid. Literature-based grammar instruction can help students think about grammar as a way to grow as writers, readers, and learners. Best of luck to you and your students as you use this book to embark on the journey of innovative grammar instruction. Know that countless works of literature (including those discussed in this book) support you as you help your students think metacognitively about grammar.

References

Anderson, J. (2005). *Mechanically inclined*. Portland, ME: Stenhouse.

Avi. (1998). *Perloo the bold*. New York, NY: Scholastic.

Barone, D. M., Xu, S. H., & Mallette, M. H. (2005). *Teaching early literacy: Development, assessment, and instruction* (2nd ed.). New York, NY: Guilford Press.

Babbitt, N. (1975). *Tuck everlasting*. New York, NY: Farrar, Straus and Giroux.

Barnett, M. (2012). *It happened on a train*. New York, NY: Simon & Schuster Books for Young Readers.

Beck, I., McKeown, M., Hamilton, R., & Kucan, L. (1997). *Questioning the author: An approach for enhancing student engagement with text*. Newark, DE: International Reading Association.

Biber, D. (1995). *Dimensions of register variation: A cross-linguistic comparison*. Cambridge, UK: Cambridge University Press.

Bratcher, S., & Ryan, L. (2004). *Evaluating children's writing* (2nd ed.). Mahwah, NJ: Lawrence Earlbaum Associates.

Brooks. B. (2000). *Throwing smoke*. New York, NY: HarperCollins.

Brown, J. (1983). *Flat Stanley: Stanley and the magic lamp*. New York, NY: HarperCollins.

Byars, B., Duffey, B., & Myers, L. (2004. *The SOS file*. New York, NY: Henry Holt & Co.

Christopher, M. (1989). *Catch that pass*. Boston, MA: Little, Brown, and Company.

Christopher, M. (1990). *Top wing*. Boston, MA: Little, Brown, and Company.

Cleary, B. (1982). *Ralph S. Mouse*. New York, NY: HarperCollins.

Cleary, B. (1983). *Dear Mr. Henshaw*. New York, NY: Scholastic.

Common Core State Standards Initiative. (2010). Common core state standards for English language arts. Retrieved from http://www.corestandards.org/ELA-Literacy.

Connors, R. J., & Lunsford, A. A. (1988). Frequency of formal errors in current college writing, or ma and pa do kettle research. *College Composition and Communication*, 39(4), 395–409.

Creech, S. (1994). *Walk two moons*. New York, NY: HarperCollins.

Dahl, R. (1980). *The twits*. New York, NY: Puffin.

De Saint-Exupery, A. (1943). *The little prince*. Boston, MA: Harcourt.

DiCamillo, K. (2000). *Because of Winn-Dixie*. Cambridge, MA: Candlewick Press.

DiCamillo, K. (2006). *The miraculous journey of Edward Tulane*. Cambridge, MA: Candlewick Press.

Fisher, D., & Frey, N. (2003). Writing instruction for struggling adolescent readers: A gradual release model. *Journal of Adolescent and Adult Literacy, 46*(5), 396–407.

Flavell, J. H. (1979). Metacognition and cognitive monitoring. *American Psychologist, 34*, 906–911.

Fleischman, P. (1997). *Seedfolks*. New York, NY: Harper Trophy.

Fletcher, R., & Portalupi, J. (2001). *Writing workshop: The essential guide*. Portsmouth, NH: Heinemann.

Gantos, J. (2000). *Joey Pigza loses control*. New York, NY: Farrar, Straus and Giroux.

Garner, R. (1987). *Metacognition and reading comprehension*. Norwood, NJ: Ablex.

Hale, B. (2001). *The big nap*. Boston, MA: Harcourt.

Hall, J. H. (Ed.). (2002). *Dictionary of American regional English*. Cambridge, MA: Belknap Press of Harvard University Press.

Hamilton, V. (1999). *Bluish*. New York, NY: Scholastic.

Henkes, K. (1997). *Sun & spoon*. New York, NY: Puffin.

Herron, C. (1998). *Nappy hair*. New York, NY: Dragonfly Books.

Hiaasen, C. (2012). *Chomp*. New York, NY: Knopf Books for Young Readers.

Killgallon, D., & Killgallon, J. (2010). *Grammar for college writing: A sentence-composing approach*. Portsmouth, NH: Heinemann.

Kinney, J. (2007). *Diary of a wimpy kid*. New York, NY: Amulet Books.

Kinney, J. (2009). *Diary of a wimpy kid: The last straw*. New York, NY: Amulet Books.

Kolln, M. & Funk, R. (2009). *Understanding English grammar* (8th ed.) New York, NY: Pearson.

Korman, G. (1989). *Radio fifth grade*. New York, NY: Scholastic.

Korman, G. (2001). *Shipwreck*. New York, NY: Scholastic.

Lasky, K. (2006). *The Coming of Hoole*. New York, NY: Scholastic.

Lasky, K. (2010). *Chasing Orion*. Somerville, MA: Candlewick Press.

Lindgren, A. (1950). *Pippi Longstocking*. New York, NY: Viking Press.

Lloyd, S. L. (2004). Using comprehension strategies as a springboard for student talk. *Journal of Adolescent and Adult Literacy, 48*(2), 114–124.

Lupica, M. (2010). *The batboy*. New York, NY: Puffin Books.

Lyman, F. (1987). Think-pair-share: An expanding teaching technique. *MAA-CIE Cooperative News, 1*(1), 1–2.

MacNeil, R., & Cran, W. (2005). *Do you speak American?* Boston, MA: Houghton Mifflin Harcourt.

McDonald, M. (2005). *Stink: The incredible shrinking kid*. Somerville, MA: Candlewick Press.

McKissack, P. (1992). *A million fish . . . more or less*. New York, NY: Dragonfly Books.

McKissack, P. (1986). *Flossie and the fox*. New York, NY: Dial Books for Young Readers.

Mayher, J. S. (1989). *Uncommon sense: Theoretical practice in language education*. Portsmouth, NH: Heinemann.

National Council of Teachers of English (2004). NCTE beliefs about the teaching of writing. Retrieved from http://www.ncte.org/positions/statements/writingbeliefs.

Osborne, M. P. (1996). *Sunset of the sabertooth*. New York, NY: Random House.

Paulsen, G. (1987). *Hatchet*. New York, NY: Simon & Schuster.

Pearson, P. D., & Gallagher, M. C. (1983). The instruction of reading comprehension. *Contemporary Educational Psychology, 8*, 317–344.

Peck, R. (1995). *Lost in cyberspace*. New York, NY: Puffin.

Repanich, J. (2012). The new powers. *Sports Illustrated for Kids, 24*(7), 20–23.

Robb, L. (2001). *Grammar lessons and strategies that strengthen students' writing*. New York, NY: Scholastic.

Rockwell, T. (1973). *How to eat fried worms*. New York, NY: Yearling.

Rowling, J. K. (1997). *Harry Potter and the sorcerer's stone*. New York, NY: Scholastic.

Sachar, L. (1985). *Sideways stories from wayside school*. New York, NY: HarperCollins.

Sharmat, M. W., & Sharmat, M. (2004). *Nate the great on the owl express*. New York, NY: Yearling.

Sharpe, S. (1990). *Trouble at marsh harbor*. New York, NY: Scholastic.

Sobol, D. (1982). *Encyclopedia Brown sets the pace*. New York, NY: Scholastic.

Sobol, D. (1994). *Encyclopedia Brown and the case of the two spies*. New York, NY: Scholastic.

Spinelli, J. (1990). *Maniac Magee*. Boston, MA: Little, Brown, and Company.

Spinelli, J. (1996). *Crash*. New York, NY: Random House.

Stamper, J. (2003). *Magic School Bus: Voyage to the volcano*. New York, NY: Scholastic.

Truss, L. (2003). *Eats, shoots and leaves*. New York, NY: Gotham Books.

Weaver, C. (1998). Teaching grammar in the context of writing. In C. Weaver (Ed.), *Lessons to share on teaching grammar in context* (pp. 18–38). Portsmouth, NH: Boynton/Cook.

Wheeler, R., & Swords, R. (2006). *Code-switching: Teaching standard English in urban classrooms*. Urbana, IL: National Council of Teachers of English.

White, E. B. (1952). *Charlotte's web*. New York, NY: HarperCollins.

Wolfram, W., & Schilling-Estes, N. (1998). *American English: Dialects and variation*. Malden, MA: Blackwell.

Woltjer, S. (1998). Facilitating the use of description—and grammar. In C. Weaver (Ed.), *Lessons to share on teaching grammar in context* (pp. 95–99). Portsmouth, NH: Boynton/Cook.